Scribble Art

Scribble Art

INDEPENDENT PROCESS ART EXPERIENCES FOR CHILDREN

MaryAnn F. Kohl

CHICAGO
REVIEW
PRESS

Published by Chicago Review Press Incorporated
814 North Franklin Street
Chicago, Illinois 60610
ISBN 978-1-64160-840-4

Library of Congress Cataloging-in-Publication Data
Is available from the Library of Congress.

Cover and interior design: Jonathan Hahn
Cover photographs: (front cover, left to right) Courtesy Kylie D'Alton, Emma Koehler,
   Trisha Thompson, and Carey LaMothe; (back cover, left to right) Courtesy Emma
   Koehler, Zannifer Gail, Jennifer Crowell, MaryAnn Kohl

Printed in China
5 4 3 2 1

Dedication

In memory of Michael L. Kohl

About the Photographs

All the photographs of children and art activities in this book were captured organically and naturally as children were working and creating in their normal environments. Children were never asked to pose, although some children specifically requested to have their photographs taken with their art. No professional photographs of children as models or commercial photographs were used at any time. Attention was given to diversity, age, and gender. All photographs have been printed with permission by each owner. All rights are reserved, and no reprints are allowed without permission from MaryAnn Faubion Kohl through her website at brightring.com /contact-us.

Acknowledgments

Thank you to all the teachers and parents from our online art group, Process Art with MaryAnn Kohl, who brought inspiring photographs to this book. Thank you for your expertise with young children, your caring hearts, and your hard work. That includes friends and family who pitched in for *Scribble Art*! I give each of you my deepest appreciation and thanks. You made this book come to life.

Adele Price
Amy Kay
Ana Dziengel, Babble Dabble Do
Andrea Diuguid
Andrea Reeves
Anna Ranson, Imagination Tree
Barbara Rucci, Art Bar
Bonita Sears
Brenda Marsden
Brittany Dusek
Caitlin Rot
Carey LaMothe
Carrie Bryant
Cathy Bode

Catie Schnieder
Cheryl Uy
Children's Museum of Pittsburgh
Christie Burnett
Christine Kellerman
Cindi Frakes Zieger
Cristy Ward
Demaris Weitzel
Emma Koehler
Erin DeThomas
Heather Ann Goodman
Janine Kloiber
Jansi Rani
Jeanette Wheeler Strom

Jeanne Elser Smith
Jennifer Goodman Crowell
Julie Dugger
Karen Begley
Kelly Hinds
Kim Solga
Kylie D'Alton
Larissa Halfond
Linda Tandy
Mary Turner
Megan Collins
Megan Harney
Megan Hunter Scarmazzi
Megan Kohl

Melea Martin
Melissa Jordan
Michelle Rasmussen
Natalie Valentine
Nia Jones
Rachelle Doorley, TinkerLab
Ronda Harbaugh
Sue Gaudnyski
Suzanne Cotton
Tricia Lynn Carpenter
Trisha Thompson
Vidya Rao
Wheaton Arts
Zannifer Rolich

"Every time we teach a child something, we keep him from inventing it himself. On the other hand, that which we allow him to discover for himself, will remain with him visible for the rest of his life."

—John Piaget

"Art is a place for children to learn to trust their own ideas, themselves, and to explore what is possible."

—MaryAnn Faubion Kohl

Letter to the Young Artist

Hello, Young Artist:

I'm so happy to meet you! Are you ready to enter the world of creativity, where there is no right or wrong way to create? Imagine feeling free to encounter any art experience without a set of rules or expectations for outcomes! I like to say, "It's the process not the product," which means the important part of art is the doing—exploring, creating, discovering, experimenting, and attempting of new ideas. The final product or how the art turns out is fun too, but the true focus is what you learn and enjoy while exploring, experimenting, and discovering. Yes, really! Rather than working toward the end product of art as a goal, the process of making art takes priority. There is no copying an adult's art sample or making your art look like a friend's. You are independent and doing your own thing. You, the artist, need only please yourself.

Think of art explorations as science experiments. Try new ideas! See what happens! Learn from exploring and discovering. Some art will look great and some may not, but what you discover in the process is worth so much more than perfect-looking results. Even so, I can promise you that you will see amazing creations that will surprise and delight.

I hope you will enjoy creating and discovering as you drip, smudge, glop, and sculpt your way through this book. Oh, I almost forgot. Remember to tidy up after creating, and observe safety at all times.

Your artsy friend,
MaryAnn Faubion Kohl

Contents

Introduction

What Is Process Art?

Process art is art for children that values exploring, discovering, and experimenting with art materials. Materials are independently available or offered in an area where the child can explore materials freely and without time limit. Creating in this way has no planned outcome and no adult sample to copy. There are no expectations for a finished product, though many final outcomes will be exciting, interesting, or beautiful—and all will be unique. Like snowflakes, no two process art experiences will ever be identical, even if the same materials are used by children working closely. This is because children create process art with individual and unique choices they make with materials on hand and the focus is the experience, not the outcome. Process art is developmentally appropriate and important because children are developing and exploring at their own pace and skill level and are learning to trust their own ideas.

Process Art Versus Crafts: What's the Difference?

The terms *process art* and *crafts* are often used interchangeably to describe the same activities for children, but they actually have important differences in their implementation and learning implications. Because art and crafts are so different, it's good to know what makes them unique and call them by their proper names.

What most adults call crafts are anything a child makes or creates: craft time at the library, crafts at camp, crafts in school, crafts at church or synagogue, craft corner at home, or the craft area at daycare. Crafts involve the child reproducing an adult's idea while following directions to make a specific thing that is a known outcome. Crafts are meant to be useful or practical, or to reinforce a fact or learning theme. Craft activities have value in this way.

Process art is the unique form of creativity that inspires each individual child to be original and inventive and to think for themselves. When children create process art, they are exploring, discovering, and thinking. Art encourages a child's originality and unique expression with an unknown outcome.

PROCESS ART	PRODUCT CRAFTS
Child Driven	**Adult Driven**
• Focus is on learning	• Focus is on adult's ideas or lesson
• No model or sample for child to copy	• Child replicates a model or sample as a directed outcome
• Open-ended process and outcome	• Closed activity and outcome
• Exploration, experimentation, and discovery with art materials, no directions to follow	• Step-by-step directions with specific materials
• Art results are spontaneous and unpredictable	• Activity and results are predictable and adult planned
• Child decides what and how to create their own artworks	• Adult decides how and what to accomplish as the end product

The Icons

Positioned in the upper outside corner of each art experience page are icons that help the parent, teacher, or artist evaluate that particular project as to art technique, experience level, adult prep and planning, basic art activities, caution needed, or help needed.

Art Technique

The art icon indicates which art medium or technique is the primary focus of the art activity:

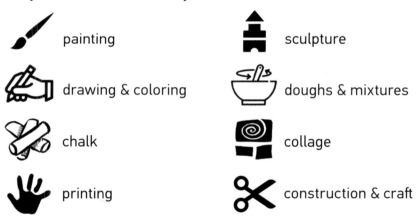

painting

sculpture

drawing & coloring

doughs & mixtures

chalk

collage

printing

construction & craft

Experience Level

The experience icon is to assist in choosing, not to limit children from choosing. Age and skill do not necessarily go hand and hand. Therefore, the experience icon flags which projects are for new or beginning-level artists, which are for mid-level artists with some experience, and which are for advanced-level artists with greater experience. However, all children can explore all projects whether the skill level matches their own or not. They may just need a little extra help.

To help make the selection of art projects more precise and to help match skill levels of children, the projects are labeled with icons of:

 1 star—for beginning artists with little experience (easiest or beginner)

 2 stars—for artists with some art experience (intermediate or moderate)

 3 stars—for the more experienced artist (advanced or complex)

Planning & Preparation

The planning and preparation icon indicates the degree of involvement and time for the adult in charge.

easy   moderate   involved

Basic Art

 Some art experiences are fundamental or basic to some or all other projects. For instance, finger painting is fundamental to finger paint monoprinting. Doing a basic finger

painting before the monoprint will give more success, understanding, and experience to the monoprint. Art ideas that are basic should be experienced by all children for a well-balanced art program and are marked with an apple. These art experiences should not be missed and can be repeated over and over.

Caution

 When electrical, sharp, hot, or adult tools are used in a project, the caution sign indicates that extra care and close supervision are necessary for the child. An adult should do the more difficult steps or assist the artist carefully.

Help

An art activity marked with this icon may not be dangerous or require extra caution but may require assistance from another child or another person.

Basic Art Materials

The following list of suggested art materials provides well-rounded choices for any art program at home, in childcare, or at school. Collect and purchase what you can. Friends and family will save things for you if you ask. Buying in bulk can save money, and collecting free materials can build a rich supply of art supplies.

Materials marked with an asterisk are the most basic and necessary supplies for children to begin exploring important and fundamental art experiences.

*art tissue: Art tissue paper comes in many colors and can be purchased in packs of one color or a mixture of colors. Look for "bleeding" art tissue, not lightweight gift wrap tissue. Bleeding art tissue releases its color when wet, just like crepe paper.

brayer: A roller especially designed for making prints. A rolling pin can also be used.

butcher paper: Heavy-gauge paper on wide rolls available from school supply stores in many colors. Great for many art projects.

cardboard: Many uses. Primarily for sculpture or as the base for other projects.

coffee filters: Useful for art ideas involving dyeing with food coloring, powdered vegetable dye, or watercolor paint.

*collage items: See the list of collage items on page 140 for detailed, alphabetical suggestions. Items to save for collage range from paper scraps to jewelry.

colored chalk: Look for soft, bright chalk that is not scratchy or labeled "for chalkboards only." Sometimes called chalk pastels.

contact paper, clear: Clear plastic with pull-away backing. Contact paper sticks to almost all surfaces. Use to cover paper to save designs or as the art surface.

*crayons: Crayola is still the best, but any crayons will do. Keep stubs, peel them, and use for additional crayon projects.

darning needle, plastic: Young children can use these for sewing and stitching with yarn on cardboard, Styrofoam trays, or other materials and fabrics. Has large eye and is not as sharp as regular needles.

embroidery floss: Useful for all projects that ask for yarn or thread. Rainbow of colors. Expensive but scraps can be gathered from many people for a nice selection.

*fabric scraps: Save all types of fabric scraps for art such as gluing to paper or cardboard, sewing, weaving, or other decorating uses.

*felt pens (marking pens): Come in many styles and qualities, from fine tip to broad, from water based to permanent. Good pens last the longest. Permanent markers should be supervised because they really are permanent!

*flour, salt, cornstarch, baking soda: Useful for many dough and playdough recipes as well as homemade paste, paint, and other glazes. See the recipe section of this book for suggestions.

*food coloring, liquid: Substitute in most projects that require paint or dye. Good for paper dyeing, dough coloring, and printing projects.

food coloring, paste: Use in same projects as liquid food coloring, but it is more concentrated and goes farther than liquid. Use in art calling for powdered vegetable dye.

framing scraps: Framing shops have a multitude of wooden framing scraps available for free. Provide the framer with a box and the framer will fill it with scraps covered in gold, fabric, carvings, and other wonderful designs.

*glitter: Store in a salt or cheese shaker. Excess glitter can be collected and poured back into the shaker, or a new container for mixed colors.

glue, tacky (hobby): Tacky glue is thicker and stickier than white glue. Especially useful for fabric gluing.

*glue, white: Usually known as Elmer's School Glue or, in Canada, Le Page's Glue. A basic for a plethora of art activities. Can be thinned with water and used as a glaze or used for gluing paper and other materials.

glue gun: To be used only with adult supervision or by the adult for quick, solid gluing. Never leave a child unattended with a glue gun. New cool glue guns are suitable for younger children with supervision.

hole punch (paper punch): Useful for punching holes in cardboard, paper, tagboard, and other materials. The holes from the punch are also useful as confetti and other decoration. Invest in a heavy-duty punch for punching holes in thick paper, several layers of paper, or poster board. Craft punches are similar and come in shapes such as hearts and holiday symbols.

ink pad: For printing with rubber stamps or self-designed stamps made of other materials. Come in many colors. Refill bottles can be purchased to reink a dry pad.

iron (old): An old iron comes in handy for many art projects such as melting crayon between waxed paper pieces or transferring crayon designs from paper to fabric. Also good for flattening curled paintings.

*liquid watercolors: Bright and strong colors in bottles with pouring spouts. Can be thinned. These have become a staple of art activities for all ages.

*masking tape: Sturdy brown tape in several different widths that tears or cuts easily. Can be peeled off again from most surfaces if not left on too long. Also comes in a rainbow of colors and patterns. Blue painter's tape removes easier than brown masking tape.

*mat board: A basic supply for art, mat board can be collected for free in all shapes, colors, and sizes from framing shops. Provide the shop with a box and pick it up full of mat board every couple weeks or so.

*newsprint: Available from local printers, printers' supply stores, and newspaper printers. Also available from moving and shipping companies. Newspaper and newsprint can be used for most of the same art projects. Newspaper has words and images on it, and newsprint is plain and clean.

*oil pastels: A combination of chalk and crayon available from art or hobby stores. Brighter and less smudgy than chalk but blends better than crayon.

*paintbrushes: Brushes come in many shapes and sizes. For quality results, buy quality brushes. Most school supply stores carry some nice ones for easel and watercolor painting.

*paper: All kinds, all colors, from stores or saved from the recycle bin at printshops. Save a variety. Cut into shapes or smaller pieces. Use both sides to extend use.

*paper scraps: All papers, from junk to art paper, eventually become scraps. Save for all kinds of art projects.

paste: Paste comes in jars with brushes, is nontoxic, and works in ways glue can't. Can be mixed with paint for color.

pastels: Soft art chalk in many colors. Usually has squared edges rather than round.

pencils: Pencils come in handy when lines need to be erased, for general drawing, for tracing, and for delicate rubbings. Colored pencils are good for older children or for young children who have some experience in drawing with crayon and regular pencils.

play clay: Sometimes called Plasticine. A commercial modeling product in bright colors. Will not harden or dry out. Can stain. Useful for many art experiences.

*scissors: Don't skimp on the quality of scissors. Good, sharp scissors are a basic for children and are available with blunt ends for safety.

*stapler: Little hands can work medium to large staplers quite well. Avoid the tiny staplers. Show kids how to fill a stapler and have one less job to worry about.

starch, liquid: Use to mix paint into a smooth consistency for a glaze over paper projects or for a glue substitute. Available in the laundry section of grocery stores and in the art section of school supply stores.

Styrofoam grocery tray: Useful as the base of many art projects, as a container for paint or glue, to sort or store collage items, and to cut up for other art uses. Wash and dry before using. Some stores will donate trays or sell them for a fair price.

*tape (all kinds): Keep a supply of tape—cellophane, duct, washi, masking, library—any kinds at all. Kids never seem to have enough tape suitable for all jobs.

*tempera paint, liquid: Liquid tempera paint is usually thick enough that it still needs to be thinned with water or liquid starch before painting. Liquid tempera is more expensive than powdered but offers some convenience in that it is already mixed and generally usable.

tempera paint, powdered: Dry tempera paint has many uses and art applications and comes in many colors. If you don't have a large budget, buy the basic primary colors of paint and mix all other colors you would like from red, yellow, and blue. Buy white, too, to make pastel colors, but you can do without black.

watercolor paint: Comes in tubes, blocks, or paint boxes. Paint boxes and blocks work best for children. Use a good brush and good paper for best results.

wood scraps: Save pieces from a frame shop, shop class, or construction site for sculptures or for the base of other artwork. Can be painted, glued, nailed, or used as a printing tool.

*yarn: Save scraps of all colors, textures, and styles. Keep yarn rolled in balls and stick the loose end through a hole in a box for a yarn dispenser. Useful for weaving, hanging, or sewing.

1

Paper & Collage

 # Cut & Paste

Cutting and pasting paper is one of the most basic art experiences for artists of any age because of its open-ended possibilities and room for imagination and inventiveness. There are so many types of paper available! So many ways paper can be worked! Save junk mail. Befriend a local printshop for scraps and misprinted paper in all sizes. Keep a supply of construction paper and save the leftovers. For extra creativity and design, add collage materials (page 140) as well.

MATERIALS

Suggested papers to save and use:

art tissue	envelopes	junk mail	photos	tracing paper
brochures	file folders	lunch sacks	poster board	wallpaper
cardboard	food wrappers	magazines	posters	watercolor paper
cardstock	gift wrap tissue	mat board	rice paper	wrapping paper
catalogs	greeting cards	newspaper	stationery	
copying paper	grocery bags	paper towels	tagboard	

Suggested materials for sticking and binding paper:

brads	glue sticks	needle and thread	ribbons	string
contact paper	hole punch	paper clips	stapler	tape
duct tape	labels	paste	stickers	washi tape
glue	masking tape	pins	sticky dots	yarn

Mulberry House Playschool
Courtesy Suzanne Cotton

PROCESS

1. Provide paper of any kind and items to use for sticking and binding. Allow for complete freedom and exploration.
2. Cut and paste or stick paper to other papers.
3. Use marking tools or collage materials for additional design if desired.

EXTENSIONS

• Focus cut-and-paste art on a theme:

– alphabet	– cultures	– food	– love	– play	– travel
– animals	– emotions	– friends	– nutrition	– school	– undersea
– counting	– family	– holidays	– pets	– outer space	– wishes

Courtesy MaryAnn Kohl

Torn Paper Design

Tearing paper is a skill that precedes using scissors. But most children prefer scissors to tearing even if they have the control to tear paper the way they want it to come out. Therefore, encourage the fun, unique rough edges, and unexpected results of tearing paper. Consider allowing children to experiment with tearing before the activity of gluing a finished design is introduced. This may help them better understand the behavior of how paper tears.

MATERIALS

scraps of construction paper
scraps of other kinds of paper
sheet of paper for the base
glue or tape

PROCESS

1. Tear the paper into pieces.
2. Arrange the torn pieces on the larger sheet of background paper. Designs may be random and unplanned, or realistic and planned.
3. Glue the pieces to the background paper in a random design or a more specific scene or picture.
4. Dry completely.

EXTENSION

Other types of paper to use for torn design:

- coloring book pages
- drawings
- wrapping paper
- old greeting cards
- junk mail
- newspaper
- photographs
- posters
- used homework

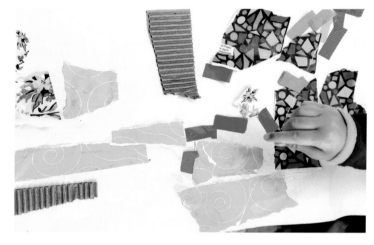

Art by Anna, age 3.
Courtesy Adele Price, 2021

Paper Collage

Courtesy MaryAnn Kohl, 2021

For artists young and old, paper collage is a universal art medium that never grows tiresome. The possibilities are always changing based on the materials on hand and the age and imagination of the artist. Collage can be flat or three dimensional as paper is versatile in its structural possibilities.

MATERIALS

glue, paste, tape
scissors
Papers and scraps:

construction paper	gift wrap tissue	magazines	posters
cupcake liners	greeting cards	napkins	wallpaper
facial tissue	grocery bags	newspaper	wrapping paper

Base material:

box	cardstock	mat board	Styrofoam tray
cardboard	file folder	paper	wood

PROCESS

1. Cut and glue paper in a random or planned approach on the selected base. Cover the entire base if desired, overlapping edges so the base does not show through.
2. Dry, overnight if needed.
3. The finished collage can be brushed with white glue to give it a shiny, clear surface.

EXTENSIONS

- Create a theme collage:
  –happiness   –friends   –holiday   –pets   –flowers   –food   –toys
- Work in a group and create a huge collage. Sneak in photographs of the individual artists.
- Cover a paper collage with clear contact paper and use for a place mat, an alphabet search, animal search, or games using washable markers.

3D Paper Experiments

Building and constructing with paper scraps has infinite possibilities, from the simple to the complex. Some artists enjoy creating a "bug playground" or a "pixie village" with curly paper to climb and loops and bends to play on. Others prefer to explore what happens and what is possible with paper that grows up and out from the base.

MATERIALS

scraps of construction paper
scraps of other kinds of paper
base material: paper plate, mat board,
    cardboard, construction paper

glue, tape, stapler
pencils, crayons, markers
hole punch

Elli Harney, age 7.
Courtesy Megan Harney, ourhandcraftedlife.com, 2021

PROCESS

1. Allow artists to experiment with paper scraps and shapes to make them stand vertically on the base paper.
2. Colorful paper on a black background is visually effective.
3. Artists may cut, tear, tape, staple, or glue scraps, or use them as they are. Possibilities are wide open.
4. Some 3D paper art techniques to explore are:

– bend	– curve	– gather	– punch	– soften	– tuft
– bow	– cut	– knot	– ridge	– spiral	– twist
– braid	– fold	– loop	– roll	– tassel	– wad
– crease	– frill	– pleat	– score	– tear	– warp
– crimp	– fringe	– plume	– scrape	– tie	– weave
– curl	– furrow	– pucker	– slit	– tuck	– wrinkle

EXTENSION

Group 3D experiment: If multiple 3D experiments are individually created, they can be joined together in one display.

Courtesy MaryAnn Kohl, 2021

Paper Strip Art

Long strips of colored paper joined together with glue or staples are versatile and interesting to work with. They can curl, loop, bend, fold, and make unusual interconnecting designs and shapes. Prepare the strips first, and begin creating when ready.

MATERIALS

strips of colored paper
scissors
glue, stapler, tape
base material:
    box lid, heavy paper plate, wood block

tempera paints and brushes, optional
collage items, optional

PROCESS

1. Cut strips of colored paper.
2. Glue or staple three to four strips together to make an even longer strip. Pieces can also be stacked together and glued to make very strong, thick strips.
3. Twist and bend the strips into interlocking shapes.
4. Glue the strips to a base. Use tape to hold the sculpture in place if needed.
5. Paint the sculpture if desired. Dry before proceeding.
6. Further design and decorate the sculpture with collage items if desired.

EXTENSIONS

- Create mobiles.
- Create party decorations such as chains, garlands, and streamers.

Art by Cassie, age 4.
Courtesy Melissa Jordan, thechocolatemuffintree.blogspot.com, 2021

Cut Paper Design

Who remembers making snowflakes with all the little cuts, holes, and leftover snips? Cut paper design builds on this concept but adds other dimensions. Artists should explore folding any shape of paper into any pattern and then cutting larger or more numerous holes. The idea is to leave less paper and more holes. Save the scraps for other art ideas.

MATERIALS

copying paper or patterned craft paper
scissors
colored paper for base, optional
glue

PROCESS

1. Fold a sheet of paper into a small square, triangle, or other shape.
2. Cut shapes, holes, slits, and designs from the folds of the paper until there is very little paper remaining. Cut big, bold holes! (Save the snipped paper for other projects.)
3. Carefully unfold the cut paper design. Consider adding more cut paper designs to the artwork.
4. Glue the design down on a background of colored paper, if desired, or leave as is.

EXTENSIONS

- Join several cut designs on one background paper.
- Try to cut a star, heart, flower, or apple. The shape can be further folded, and holes cut from it.
- Mount the cut design on a background of patterned craft paper, wrapping paper, an old poster, or original drawings. The colors and designs will show through the bold cuts and holes.

Art by child, age 10.
Courtesy Brenda Marsden, 2021

Scored Paper

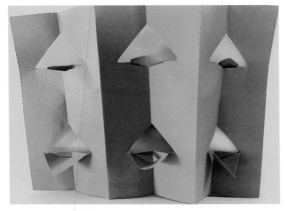

Scored paper is made by cutting little holes, slits, and shapes, which can then be folded out or cut away. With this technique, artists can create sculptures ranging from a snowflake to a complex architectural design with spires and windows.

MATERIALS

copying paper
scissors (various sizes and edge designs)
hole punch
ruler, optional
pencil, optional

crayons or markers, optional
tape, glue, or stapler, optional
hobby knife, used only with careful adult supervision, optional

Courtesy MaryAnn Kohl, 2021

PROCESS

1. Cut designs into paper with the various cutting tools. Paper may be folded, punctured, or handled in any way the artist chooses. Some artists first draw lightly with a pencil to decide where to cut or use a ruler to find straight lines.
2. When cuts, slits, holes, or other designs have been cut, the cut paper sections can be folded out or scored to stand away from the paper.
3. When a design is complete, the paper may be further decorated with crayons or markers. Artists may continue to add more design ideas with tape, glue, or staples.

EXTENSION

- Stand a scored, cut, and completed paper design on one edge and form it into a roll. Tape the loose ends together to resemble a lantern. Place an electric candle inside the lantern and see the lights shine through the scored and cut designs.

Sprinkle Dots

What is it about sprinkling confetti on glue that pleases young artists so much? This easy-to-do art requires little expertise or supplies but is always an intriguing way to introduce the process of sprinkling and gluing. Make your own dots with a hole punch, or purchase bags of commercial craft dots made from plastic, ribbons, or paper.

MATERIALS

sheet of paper for base
white glue, thinned with water in a cup
paintbrush
confetti

tiny scraps
punch dots saved from a hole punch
toothpick, optional

PROCESS

1. Mix 1 part water to 2 parts white glue in a container. Brush some thinned glue over part of the base paper.
2. Sprinkle or place confetti on the sticky areas. Some artists like to use a toothpick to move the dots around. Other artists like to "pour" dots on the glue.
3. Shake off excess dots and confetti onto a separate piece of paper to use again.
4. Brush with more thinned glue. Proceed until the base paper is covered in a desired design.
5. Allow art to dry completely.

EXTENSIONS

- Follow the sprinkle dot technique on a block of wood, mat board, waxed paper, rock, or other base of choice.
- Sprinkle dots are effective when glued on a drawing or painting to resemble stars, snow, magic, the night sky, or celebrations.
- Explore creating with other bits and pieces:
  - art tissue scrap
  - paper scraps
  - pebbles
  - sand
  - sewing scraps

Art by Ivy, age 2.
Courtesy Janine Kloiber, 2021

 # Crepe Paper Canvas

Young artists explore blending the bright colors of crepe paper on a craft canvas. Adding water releases the dye in the crepe paper, causing colors to blend and mix.

MATERIALS

white glue and water
container for mixing water and glue
small flat container or tray
roller, paintbrush, or sponge

craft canvas (any size)
crepe paper, 2 or more colors
scissors

PROCESS

1. Mix 1 part water to 2 parts white glue in a container. Mix and stir with a paintbrush until well combined.
2. Brush the entire canvas with the glue-water mixture. One good technique is to pour a little of the glue mixture in a flat container that fits the roller. If you don't have a roller, a paintbrush will do.
3. Cut or tear lengths of crepe paper. Pieces can be torn into any sizes the artist chooses. Press each one on the canvas.
4. Cover the roller (or paintbrush or sponge) in the glue-water mixture, and then roll glue over each one as placed.
5. Add a little extra water with a brush to encourage the crepe paper to release its dye.
6. When done, dry the canvas completely overnight. A few hours of drying is usually enough.

EXTENSIONS

- Bleeding art tissue can be substituted in any crepe paper art experience, and vice versa.
- Brush crepe paper pieces on a sheet of cardstock using water only. The pieces can be pulled away, leaving stains on the paper.

Art by Quinn, age 3.
Courtesy Andrea Reeves, KinderMarlee Early Childhood Centre, 2021

Magazine Collé

A collé is similar to a collage. Using magazine or catalog pictures, create a new way of looking at an object or face. For instance, a magazine picture of a woman's brown hair could be cut and pasted in a collé to resemble brown fields. A cutout of a bagel could be arranged to resemble an island in the sea. Although this is a somewhat abstract idea, artists catch on quickly. Humor is to be expected.

MATERIALS

colorful magazine and catalog
   pictures
scissors

paste or glue
sheet of paper for base
crayons or markers, optional

PROCESS

1. Select a magazine picture to cut and then be used as texture for a drawing or design. For instance, a magazine picture of a field of wheat could be used as the fur for a lion. Or a magazine picture of a strawberry in a bowl of cereal could be used as the nose of a puppy.
2. Cut the magazine pictures into shapes that can create a scene or design or be part of a drawing. Arrange them on the base paper.
3. When ready paste down the magazine shapes.
4. Add drawings with crayon or pen to enhance the design if desired.

Courtesy MaryAnn Kohl, 2021

EXTENSIONS

- Cover the entire background paper with magazine pictures in a collage.
- Paste magazine picture shapes on paper to represent a favorite color or theme:
  - cut-out flowers pasted to resemble one larger flower
  - blue magazine cutouts to make an all-blue collage
  - seasonal or holiday cutouts to create a festively themed scene

Shapes upon Shapes

Art by Hilde, age 2.
Courtesy MaryAnn Kohl, 2021

Choose one shape to feature in this colorful collage—for example, circles. Cut a variety of sizes of that one shape. Then glue them all piece by piece on a base paper.

MATERIALS

construction paper in several colors
scissors
suggested objects to use as templates:
    jar lid, box, bowl, ruler

pencil or pen
glue
sheet of paper for base

PROCESS

1. Depending on the child's age, either supply a tray full of precut paper in one chosen shape, such as a circle, or have kids cut out their own choice of a shape in many sizes.
2. Choose just one shape for this activity: triangle, square, rectangle, octagon, hexagon, or other. Cut the chosen shape in sizes big, medium, little, and tiny. An object can be traced to make shapes; for example, use a jar lid to make circles or a box to make a square. Finding different sizes of templates to trace is optional but inspires the direction and possibilities of the art.
3. Glue shapes on the background paper. Gluing one on top of another is perfectly fine! Explore gluing shapes and creating a paper full of overlapping colors all of one shape.

EXTENSIONS

- Trace a shape over and over on a sheet of paper (see page 13), allowing the lines to overlap. Then color in the overlapping shapes with chalk, colored pencils, crayons, or paint.
- Cut strips of colored paper and cover a canvas or square of plywood with the strips. Use a lot of glue to help them stick. Overlapping the strips and covering the background is encouraged.

Tracing Shapers

Simply tracing shapes and coloring in traced shapes is a good skill and a satisfying activity. For an added dynamic, the effect of tracing an object over and over with a slight movement of the shape each time may produce the optical illusion of the object moving quickly before the eyes. Each artist can create one's own shape to be traced.

MATERIALS

copying paper for the base
shapes cut from heavier paper
scissors

tape
pencils, crayons, markers
tempera paint and brushes, optional

PROCESS

1. Tape the base paper to the table to give stability and prevent the paper from wiggling.
2. Choose any shape and place one on the paper. (Some artists prefer to use several different shapes, not just one.)
3. Trace around the shape with a drawing tool such as a crayon, holding the shape in place with the nondrawing hand.
4. Move the shape slightly and trace again, overlapping the designs.
5. Continue tracing the shape in different positions until satisfied.
6. Color the design in any way. Use one type of coloring tool or combine several, such as markers and pencils together or crayons and markers together. Paint is also an option.

EXTENSIONS

- Create crayon rubbings (see pages 29, 30, and 85) by placing the cut shape under the paper and rubbing with a crayon to reveal the hidden shape.
- Create chalk smudging (page 38) by tracing the shapes with chalk and then brushing the chalk with cotton balls or makeup pads to blend and blur the colors.

Art by Miles LaMothe, age 10.
Courtesy Carey LaMothe, 2021

Fabric Collage

Courtesy MaryAnn Kohl and Jeanette Strom, 2021

Save fabric scraps in all textures, patterns, colors, and types. Silky, bumpy, bright, or pastel, all fabric scraps are welcome. On a piece of thick cardboard, use pushpins to attach the scraps in a collage to the cardboard. Learning to pin is a great skill for artists to explore. No pins? Simply glue the scraps on the cardboard backing.

MATERIALS

fabric scraps
sharp fabric scissors
base material in any size:
  cardboard sheet or box
  Styrofoam plate
  poster board

pushpins
glue, optional: white glue, tacky glue, fabric
  glue
wet sponge, optional

PROCESS

1. Present artists with a variety of fabric scraps. Scraps may be used as is or cut into other shapes and pieces. Younger artists may need practice cutting fabric as it is more difficult than paper. Good, sharp scissors will be required for any age.
2. Artists who are past the phase of swallowing small objects can explore pinning "fabric scraps to a thick sheet of cardboard or a cardboard box. Use the pushpins with large plastic heads to attach the scraps. Overlapping scraps will cover most of the backing.
3. In addition to (or instead of) pins, apply glue to smooth down rough edges or attach pieces of fabric. Using fingers to spread glue is often the best method. Keep a wet sponge handy for wiping sticky fingers.

EXTENSIONS

- Glue small squares of fabric scraps around the edge of an artwork as a frame.
- Read Faith Ringgold's book *Tar Beach* and recreate the fabric scraps in her illustrations.
- Staple or stitch fabric scraps on a long strand of twine to create a banner.

Tube Collage Construct

Cardboard tubes have been a staple of arts and crafts activities for generations. Incorporate tubes, carboard scraps, and other collage materials to build a structure that just might be a great place for rolling marbles or driving toy cars, or for elves or bugs to play in.

MATERIALS

flat cardboard box
cardboard tubes
cardboard scraps
paper scraps
pipe cleaners
white glue
pencil or markers
scissors
tempera paints and brushes

tape: colored masking tape, duct tape, regular tape, packing tape
collage materials, especially those with holes, cylinders, or tubes: drinking straws, small paper cups, hardware nuts and washers, film canisters, aluminum foil
small containers, empty and clean
old towel

PROCESS

1. Think about how to fill the flat cardboard box. Will it be a random collage? Will it be a planned design? Will it be a playground for tiny elves, a rolling marble maze, or a toy-car racing box? Some artists prefer to get started before they know what their collage is all about. Others choose to plan.
2. Begin the collage by gluing a cardboard tube inside the box base. It can be standing or laying down. Add more tubes as needed. Add cardboard scraps too. These can be bent into walls or platforms.
3. Drinking straws can be joined to each other by pinching one end of the first straw and inserting it into a second straw. Straws can be threaded on chenille stems (pipe cleaners) too.
4. Add other items of choice such as paper cups, film canisters, washers, and bottles.
5. When ready, the collage can be painted with tempera paints or left as is. Keep a jar of water handy for rinsing brushes, and an old towel for catching drips.
6. The collage should dry for an hour or so before carrying it or using it. White glue needs time to dry. Tempera paints dry more quickly than glue.

Art by Joe, age 8; James, age 4; and Jack, age 9.
Courtesy Sue Gaudnyski, Art in MissG's Garden, 2021.

Tissue Blossoms

Art tissue is a versatile medium with many creative applications. Creating with leftover art tissue from other projects makes good use of scraps. Artists experience fluffy, puffy art from otherwise flat tissue. Other thin papers work for this activity as well, such as magazine pages and wrapping paper.

MATERIALS

art tissue scraps or squares
pencil with an eraser
white glue in a dish

base material: paper, mat board, cardboard, paper plate
other thin scraps of paper, optional
scissors, optional

PROCESS

1. Push a square or small piece of art tissue around the eraser end of a pencil.
2. Holding the tissue around the eraser with fingertips, dab the tissue into the white glue. Then dab onto a base material such as a piece of paper or mat board, cardboard, or paper plate.
3. Continue adding tissue blossoms and filling the base with fluffy color. Other types of paper blossoms can be added if desired.
4. Dry completely.

EXTENSIONS

- Fill in a predrawn design with tissue blossom.
- Do a large group project with many hands contributing blossoms.
- For a very large blossom artwork, any types of paper can be pushed around a dowel, can, or jar and dipped into glue in a large bowl or tray. Incorporate cupcake liners for contrast and texture.

Art by Breanna Bode, age 6.
Courtesy Cathy Bode, 2021

Art Tissue & Water Collage

Liquid starch or water and bleeding art tissue are the perfect combination for an art experience that is basic and important. This activity works well for all ages. Artists apply colored tissue scraps and shapes to paper with brushed-on liquid starch, creating an artwork that is bright and aesthetically pleasing. Older artists may wish to cut the tissue into specific shapes and objects to create a more intricate work. No glue is needed! Color-mixing surprises are guaranteed. Art tissue is commercially called "bleeding art tissue" because the dye in the tissue can be released with liquids like water, thinned white glue, or liquid starch.

Courtesy Tinkerlab, Rachelle Doorley, 2021

MATERIALS

liquid starch in a dish
paintbrush
base paper: copying paper, construction paper, waxed paper, paper plate
art tissue scraps, torn pieces or squares

thinned white glue, optional (if you can't find liquid starch)

Courtesy MaryAnn Kohl, 2021

PROCESS

1. Paint liquid starch over a small area of the paper base.
2. Stick a piece of art tissue to the starched area.
3. Paint over the piece with more starch to soak through and stick all edges to the paper.
4. Continue repeating these steps. Watch for color mixing.
5. Cover the entire piece of paper as desired, overlapping pieces so the base paper does not show through. Some artists prefer to cover less of the base, which is also effective.
6. Dry the art completely to a bright, shiny finish.

EXTENSIONS

- Cut art tissue into shapes, scenes, or figures. Stick to waxed paper or plastic wrap with starch or thinned white glue.
- Cut snowflake shapes in different colors of art tissue and overlap them, sticking to clear plastic wrap with liquid starch. Then press another sheet of plastic wrap over the snowflakes to seal them in between two sheets. Cut out the snowflakes and hang from threads.

Art by child, age 2.
Courtesy Anna Ranson, Imagination Tree, 2021

Framed Artwork

Now and then a very special work of art may be saved or given as a gift from the heart to someone special. This project makes an artist's chosen gift look personal and unique. And because the artist has chosen the work of art or photo, the framed result is even more special.

Art by Valerie Thompson, age 6.
Courtesy Trisha Thompson, 2021

Art by Clio, age 2.
Courtesy MaryAnn Kohl, 2021

MATERIALS

child's chosen artwork or photo to frame
frame material: mat board, scraps from a frame shop, scraps of wood, tongue depressors, cardboard, old picture frame
mat board or cardboard for the backing

glue, tape, scissors
decorating supplies: feathers, macaroni, faux flowers, buttons, shells
paint and brush
markers, glitter glue

PROCESS

1. If you don't have mat board, cut cardboard you have on hand. You might visit a local custom frame shop and ask for mat board scraps. One type comes solid in a square or rectangle; the other type comes like a frame with a hole in the center for the artwork. Both are very useful. Hint: Leave a box for the shop to save more for you.
2. Select a drawing, painting, photo, or other artwork. If one is not handy, create one!
3. Select one of the mat frames or other frame materials for size and color. Place it around the artwork and see how it looks. Try other frames and colors until you select the one you like the best.
4. Glue or tape the artwork to a solid backing (mat board, cardboard) that is about the size of the frame and the artwork. This becomes the sturdy backing.
5. Put glue on the back of the mat board frame. Press it to the artwork, framing the best parts of the design. Trim away any excess artwork.
6. Decorate the frame with choices of supplies like feathers, faux flowers, macaroni, glitter, and other collage materials on hand. Drawing or painting the frame adds a personal touch.
7. Dry the decorated frame completely.

EXTENSIONS

- Collect used frames from garage sales and thrift shops.
- Attach magnetic strips and secure the framed artwork to the refrigerator.

Paper & Threads

Identical double paper shapes are glued and sandwiched on long threads. Hang the artistic threads from the ceiling and see them twirl in the natural movement of air and breezes.

MATERIALS

scissors
thread or yarn, about 3-foot lengths
squares of construction paper, about 6 by 6 inches
other kinds of paper squares, about 6 by 6 inches

old child-made artworks (artist can give
   permission to cut their art)
glue
tape or stapler, optional

PROCESSS

1. Have long threads, strings, or yarn cut and ready to go. A good length is 3 feet. One for each artist is ideal, though some artists may want to create more than one. A small group may like working together to fill one thread.
2. Fold a square of construction paper. Cut a shape from the folded paper. It's OK to ignore the fold or use it. Both work. Now there are two identical shapes.
3. Place one shape on the table. Stretch the thread across the table and over the shape. Add some glue to the thread and the shape. Next place the identical shape over both the thread and first shape, sandwiching them together. Glue in place.
4. Let the thread and shapes dry while working onward.
5. Add more and more shapes to the thread. Fill the thread with sandwiched shapes. They may be spaced out on the thread or close together. The artist will decide.
6. When a thread is filled and dried well enough to stay together, hang it from the ceiling or other high area to see it dance and sway in the wind.

EXTENSIONS

- Further decorate paper shapes with glitter, sequins, and prints made with paint, crayons, oil pastels, collage, and so on.
- Add other items with holes to the thread and paper, such as cupcake paper liners, macaroni, and faux flowers. A hole punch will come in handy for making a hole in thinner materials.

Courtesy MaryAnn Kohl, 2021

★★ ✂ 🏰 ◔ ✋ Stuffed Paper

Young artists love creating things bigger than life. Stuffed paper gives the opportunity to create on the large scale, enjoying the process of constructing an artwork that is large but lightweight.

Art by Hadyn, age 5.
Courtesy Julie Dugger, Lionardo Art Studio, 2021

Art by Clio, age 3.
Courtesy Megan Kohl, 2021

MATERIALS

large paper, folded in half: butcher paper or craft paper on a roll
pencil
stapler
scissors
paints or markers

glitter glue
collage items, optional
glue, optional
newspaper or paper scraps
yardstick or ruler, optional
yarn and hole punch

Art by Nia Jones.
Courtesy Nia Jones, 2021

PROCESS

1. Fold a large sheet of paper in half. Butcher paper or craft paper is a good choice.
2. With a pencil, draw any shape, design, animal, or object. Draw big and bold to fill the butcher paper.
3. Staple two or three staples on each side of the paper to hold. Cut out the shape, cutting through both sheets at the same time. The staples will help hold the sheets together.
4. Paint or decorate both sides of the shape with paints, markers, sewing trims, glitter glue, or collage items of choice. Dry completely, usually overnight.
5. Now staple the shapes together all the way around, but leave an open section big enough for hands to do the stuffing.
6. Begin wadding newspaper or other paper scraps into fluffy balls of paper. Stuff these into the big shape. Push balls all the way into the farthest part of the shape first. Use a ruler or yardstick to help if necessary. When full, staple the opening closed.
7. Punch holes in the top of the shape and fit yarn through the holes so that the shape can hang from the ceiling.

EXTENSIONS

- Create a school of swimming tropical stuffed fish hanging from the ceiling.
- Create a life-size YOU by tracing your body on the butcher paper, decorating it with clothes and hair, and then stapling and stuffing "yourself."
- Instead of staples, sew through punched holes with yarn.

Newspaper Roll Sculpture ✋ ◐ ⬒ ✂ ★★

Of all the "build it big" projects, this sculpture is the favorite, bar none. There is something amazing to young artists about building something very large very quickly. They also learn in minutes about engineering and structural strength and balance. The sky is the limit for newspaper sculptures.

Courtesy WheatonArts, 2021

MATERIALS

newspaper
½-inch wooden dowel, pencil, or other stick
masking tape

collage materials, optional: yarn, stickers, feathers, ribbons

PROCESS

To Make the Paper Rolls
1. Place a sheet of newspaper on the floor.
2. Beginning at a corner, place the dowel across the corner, and roll the paper around the dowel diagonally across the paper.
3. Let the dowel fall out with one hand while holding the roll with the other hand. Tape the end corner of the paper to the roll.
4. Make a large batch of rolls before beginning the sculpture. Double sheets of paper rolled together make an extrastrong tube.

To Make the Sculpture
1. Begin by taping the end of a roll of paper to the floor.
2. Then tape another roll to the first roll. And another, and another, being thoughtful about building a strong base structure that won't fall over.

3. Keep adding rolls, bending rolls, sticking a roll inside another roll to make a longer one, and so on. Build and build, stabilizing the structure as it forms. Use as much tape as needed.
4. Add collage items, yarn, stickers, rubber bands, or whatever works to encourage color and fun.

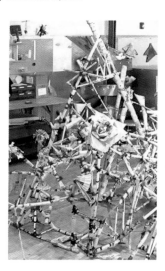

Courtesy Children's Museum of Pittsburg, 2021

EXTENSIONS
- Build a sculpture that:
  - can be entered
  - is a house
  - moves
  - is a polyhedron
  - reaches the ceiling
  - fills a room
- Use tiny squares of paper and roll them around a drinking straw or pencil to produce a smaller sculpture with the same directions.

Paper Plate Sculpture

Art by Clio, age 6.
Courtesy MaryAnn Kohl, 2021

Everyday paper plates transform into a sculpture that grows and grows. Use bright, wild designs or calm, subdued colors. The sculpture takes on a personality depending on the colors used and the shape the structure takes.

MATERIALS

paper plates (recommend using strong plates but any will work)
scissors

coloring materials: marking pens, paints and brushes, crayons
tape, optional

PROCESS

1. Cut 2-inch-deep slits in the sides of paper plates. Four slits evenly spaced around the plate are recommended. The artist can decide.
2. Choose a way to decorate the paper plates before building the sculpture. Choose to decorate both sides or one side. Some suggested ideas are:
   – draw or color bright designs or pictures with markers or crayons
   – paint designs, shapes, or pictures with paint or liquid watercolors, and let dry
3. Slip the 2-inch cut of one paper plate into the 2-inch cut of another paper plate. At this point, the plates will not stand on their own. More plates are needed!
4. Add another plate by joining one plate to another as before. Will it stand on its own yet? Plan how to add the next paper plates to encourage balance and an independent, stand-alone sculpture.
5. Continue adding plates, one to another, allowing the paper plate sculpture to grow. The size of the sculpture is ruled by how many plates there are to work with. Sometimes a little tape is needed to help things along.

EXTENSIONS

- Hang the entire paper plate sculpture from one strand of yarn.
- Build a paper plate sculpture with dessert-sized plates, or a combination of both dessert and dinner sizes.
- Hang individual colorful paper plates from strands of yarn as a bright mobile.

2

Crayon & Chalk

Free Drawing

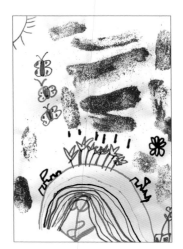

Courtesy Cheryl Uy, 2021

The best thing about free drawing is the freedom to create the unexpected and discover the boundless territory of the imagination. Experiment with the different artistic effects the following materials and tools have on drawing. Mix and match any combination in this vast area of open creativity.

Art by child, age 4.
Courtesy Ronda Harbaugh, 2021

MATERIALS

paper with differing shape, color, texture,
   thickness, absorbency
crayons: primary, jumbo, fluorescent,
   washable, peeled, shaved
paints and paintbrushes
markers, colored pencils
chalk

PROCESS

1. Try art on a variety of paper with differing textures.
2. Challenge drawing by limiting materials, such as:
   - one crayon and one paper color
   - one paintbrush, many paints
   - colored pencils and tiny paper
   - markers with opposite colored paper (red pen, green paper or blue pen, yellow paper)
3. Experience drawing on paper in different places:
   - on the wall
   - on a fence
   - hanging from a string
   - on the underside of a table
   - at the easel
   - on the floor
   - on a curved surface
   - inside a dark box
   - underwater
4. Experiment with a variety of drawing tools:
   - crayons
   - scribble cookies (p. 34)
   - chalk
   - candles or paraffin
   - charcoal
   - mulch pieces
   - pencils
   - colored pencils
   - markers
   - oil pastels
   - flower petals or weeds
   - ink

Art by Valerie, age 5.
Courtesy Trisha Thompson, 2021

EXTENSIONS

- Add scissors, glue, stapler, tape, or stickers to add to the experiment of free drawing.
- Add collage items to the free drawing.
- Incorporate magazine pictures, photographs, or cutouts as part of the free drawing.

Challenge Drawing

Create drawing or painting challenges on paper either to incorporate into a completed drawing or design or to inspire a new way of drawing.

MATERIALS

paper, prepared with challenge choice
glue
scissors
markers, crayons, or colored pencils

Art by Clio, age 6.
Courtesy MaryAnn Kohl, 2021

PROCESS

1. Use any variety of paper sizes, colors, or textures. Prepare paper with any of the following ideas:
   - cut a hole
   - draw a squiggle
   - glue on a geometric shape
   - draw or glue on a letter
   - glue on a magazine picture
2. Chose an art area: at a table, on the floor, at the easel, on the wall.
3. The artist draws on the paper challenge, trying to incorporate the shape, squiggle, hole, or letter into the drawing. Some artists choose to completely ignore or avoid the challenge. Some artists choose to work inside the challenge and leave the rest of the paper blank. Others see the possibilities of what that "thing" can be.
4. As an optional idea, an adult can take dictation of the artist's story or comments about the artwork. Writing about the artwork is in addition to the artistic experience.

Art by Hilde, age 3.
Courtesy MaryAnn Kohl, 2021

EXTENSIONS

- Artists can create challenges for a friend or family member.
- Try to look at a normal drawing and find shapes, letters, and so on that are already a part of the drawing. Hidden challenges!

Art by child, age 4.
Courtesy Zannifer Rolich, 2021

Arm Dancing

Art by child, age 5.
Courtesy Barbara Rucci, Author and Art Educator at Art Bar Blog

Art by Owen, age 3, and Jack, age 4.
Courtesy Makers, www.makersri.com, 2021

Artists draw or paint while music plays, interpreting the music in color or responding to the rhythm in stroke and design. Use large paper and find inspiring music for an exciting experience in drawing or painting to music. For added fun, a group of artists can work together on one large sheet of paper.

MATERIALS

large sheet of butcher paper
musical selection
coloring or painting tools: crayons, fingers and hands, oil pastels, paintbrushes, liquid watercolors, sponge brushes, tempera paints, marking pens

PROCESS

1. Place a large sheet of butcher paper on the floor.
2. Play a musical selection, listen, and begin to draw or paint.
3. As the music plays, artists use crayons or brushes to "arm dance" on paper. The music might motivate rhythmic drawing movements or expressions of feeling or mood. Some artists like to change colors as the mood of the music changes. Other artists use one color throughout.

TRADITIONAL MUSIC SUGGESTIONS

"In the Hall of the Mountain King" by Grieg
"Dance of the Sugar Plum Fairy" and other selections from *The Nutcracker Suite* by Tchaikovsky
"The Stars and Stripes Forever" by Sousa
1812 Overture by Tchaikovsky
"Clair de Lune" by Debussy

EXTENSIONS

- Sculpt with clay to music.
- Use Handful of Scribbles, page 27, with music.
- Enjoy any music of choice. The artists can choose favorites of their own.

Handful of Scribbles

Crayons have many uses and possibilities. A handful of crayons can be bundled together with a rubber band and used as one drawing tool with many points of color. Specific colors can be selected for the handful for a more sophisticated art experience, but the fun of a handful of a randomly selected colors is an experience of discovering and exploration.

MATERIALS

handful of crayons
strong rubber band
paper
masking tape

PROCESS

1. Wrap a rubber band around a handful of crayons that are all the same length and point size. The tips of all the crayons should be even with each other.
2. Tape a sheet of paper to the table, floor, or wall for stability.
3. Draw with the handful of crayons, experimenting with all the designs and results possible.
4. Change to a new blank sheet of large paper and repeat the drawing experience.

EXTENSIONS

- Explore using big arm movements and then very small arm movements.
- Draw with the flat ends of the crayons by turning over the handful of crayons so the opposite end of the bundle points down.
- Choose specific colors to work with—for example, gold and blue crayon on yellow paper. Experiment with combinations of colors.
- Add some cardboard shapes or other textures under the paper to add surprising rubbings to the drawing.

Art by Hilde, age 2.
Courtesy MaryAnn Kohl, 2021

Art by Raegan, age 4.
Courtesy Amy Kay, Miss Kay's Atelier, 2021

Crayon Etching

Crayon etchings can cover an entire sheet of paper or can encompass a small area within the boundaries of the paper. Starting out with a square of paper is good for beginners. The artist first covers the paper with heavy and shiny crayon color. The artist then adds a second layer of color over the first. To reveal the hidden layer, the artist scrapes through the top layer. Coloring the heavy layer of color takes patience and determination, so this activity is not for the faint of heart.

Art by Shoshana, age 12.
Courtesy MaryAnn Kohl, 2021

MATERIALS

2 or more crayons in contrasting colors
paper
facial tissue, makeup pad, or fabric scrap for
  polishing

scratching tools: paper clip (opened), bamboo
  skewer, retracting ballpoint pen with point pulled
  in, scissors points, plastic knife

PROCESS

1. Cover the surface area of the paper with a heavy, bright coat of crayon. Avoid dark colors for this first layer. Beginners should start with a smaller area of color. Color bright and strong. As young artists say, "I'm using my muscles!"
2. Color over the bright crayon layer with a dark crayon color, such as black, blue, or violet. Cover all the bright crayon, using pressure and coloring hard. This is hard work!
3. Rub the crayon surface gently with a cloth or tissue to polish and smooth the crayon.
4. Scrape the surface of dark crayon with a scratching tool, such as a scissors point, plastic knife, paper clip, or other tool. Scratch and etch through to show the bright colors below.
5. Continue etching the crayon until satisfied with the design.

Courtesy MaryAnn Kohl, 2021

EXTENSIONS

- Melt the first layer of crayon on an electric warming tray. Let the first layer harden and cool. Then add the second layer. Etch through the second layer as described.
- For the second layer, substitute crayon with a covering of black tempera paint. When the paint layer has dried, etch through the paint to the colorful crayon layer.

Hidden Crayon Rubbing

Rubbings have long been a source of beautiful art as well as a way to preserve the history of art from stone carvings, mosaics, memorials, and reliefs. Young artists explore the process of crayon rubbings through a table of hidden shapes, textures, and flat items.

MATERIALS

large sheet of butcher paper or craft paper
masking tape
peeled crayons

materials and objects to hide under the paper:
        buttons, cardboard shapes, foam shapes, keys, leaves, a license plate, paper scraps or shapes, plastic gift cards, shelf liner, tall grass blades, stencils, string or yarn

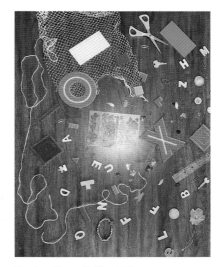

Courtesy Megan Collins, 2021

PROCESS

1. Place chosen objects on a table top. Cover the objects and the entire table with large paper. Tape to hold.
2. Rub the paper with the flat side of a peeled crayon or a scribble cookie (page 34). Surprise! Look at the designs and shapes that appear.
3. Feel about the table top to find more shapes, edges, and objects that may have been missed. Continue rubbing with crayon until satisfied.
4. Remove tape and lift the paper from the table, revealing the hidden objects.

EXTENSIONS

- Hidden crayon rubbing is a fun surprise activity for a birthday or holiday game.
- Collect natural items from outdoors for the rubbing.
- Explore rubbings with charcoal, pencil, or chalk instead of crayon.
- Head outdoors and make rubbings of tree bark, sidewalks, brick walls, fences, etc.

Art by child, age 4.
Courtesy Zannifer Rolich, 2021

Texture Rubbing

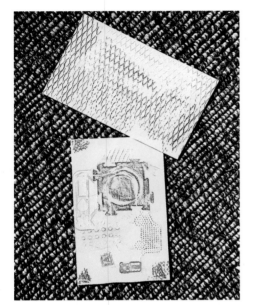

Art by Graham, age 6, and Avery, age 2.
Courtesy Caitlin Rote, 2021

Most surfaces have texture. Part of this art challenge is identifying which ones will be interesting when a crayon rubbing brings those textures to life. Hold paper over a textured surface and rub with the side of a peeled crayon or a scribble cookie (page 34). Explore tree bark, fences, screen doors, license plates, and outdoor wire or wicker furniture.

MATERIALS

peeled crayons or scribble cookies
paper
textured surfaces: tree bark, fence, screen door, basket,
    brick, license plate, wicker or wire furniture

PROCESS

1. Head outdoors with crayons and paper searching for textures.
2. When one is chosen, hold the paper over the textured surface and rub with the side of a peeled crayon or scribble cookie. If the paper is hard to hold steady, two people can work together.
3. Continue exploring textures. Try tree bark, fences, screen doors, and license plates—and don't forget to try wicker furniture piece or basket.
4. Collect the rubbings and return indoors. Look them over and see if it's possible to remember which texture rubbings came from which surface.

EXTENSIONS

- Explore hidden crayon rubbing (page 29) and tree rubbing resist (page 85).
- Explore toys for texture rubbing possibilities. For example, toy bricks make great texture rubbings with crayon.
- The kitchen has many possibilities for crayon rubbings, including a cooled rack from the oven or a bumpy tiled floor.

Art by Graham, age 6.
Courtesy Caitlin Rote, 2021

Crayon Wax Resist

When thinned tempera paint or liquid watercolors are brushed over a bright crayon drawing, the wax in the crayon resists the paint. This means the paint will not stick to the crayon but will adhere to the parts of the paper that have no crayon. Painting with a dark color over crayon marks is particularly effective for a wax resist.

MATERIALS

crayons or oil pastels, many colors
paper
thinned tempera paint, liquid watercolors, or watercolors in a paint box
paintbrush

PROCESS

1. Draw with crayon on paper. Make the marks bright, heavy, bold, and shiny. Spaces not colored will hold the most paint in step 2. Colored areas will resist the paint.
2. Brush over the crayon design with dark thinned tempera paint or watercolors. Other colors can also work well.
3. Dry completely. Hint: If the finished work curls as it dries, flatten the art by placing it between two sheets of newspaper. Press with an old iron set on low with no steam.

EXTENSIONS

- Explore drawing with paraffin or a candle. Then paint over the design as above.
- Create a design with big loops and curls of crayon. Color in the loops and shapes. Then wash over the drawing with a dark paint wash.
- Experiment with contrasts in color of paper, crayon, and paint.

Courtesy Cathy Bode, 2021

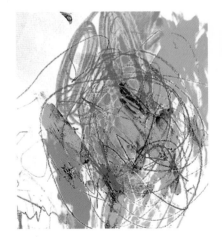

Courtesy Mary Turner, 2021

Art by Zekiel, age 4.
Courtesy Mary Turner, 2021

Oil Pastel Mini-Resist Series

(above) Courtesy Cristy Ward 2021
(right) Courtesy MaryAnn Kohl, 2021

Oil pastels have become a staple art tool for young artists to have on hand. The bright colors and thick lines are a valuable art experience, and very different from crayon or chalk. Draw with any color of oil pastels on a square of paper. Then paint over the oil pastel drawing with liquid watercolors or thinned tempera paint, which creates a resist. The artist may wish to create a series of mini-resists that can be joined together in a line or stacked in a pile and stapled to form a book.

Courtesy MaryAnn Kohl, 2021

MATERIALS

scissors
paper, white or colored, cut into 5-inch by 5-inch
    squares (other sizes are fine too)
oil pastels in many colors

liquid watercolors in small cups (or thinned
    tempera paint)
paintbrushes
tape or stapler, optional

PROCESS

1. Cut the paper into any number of squares all the same size. Squares of 5-by-5 inches work well. The artist can choose their preferred size and how many squares to make. Note: folded note cards can stand alone like little easels (see illustration).
2. Draw on one of the squares with oil pastels. Set it aside. Continue to draw on more squares, creating a series of drawings.
3. When drawings are done, spread them out on the work space. Brush over each one with liquid watercolors or thinned tempera paint. The paint will resist the oil pastels and fill in color on the paper.
4. When the series is dry, tape the drawings together in a line or stack them in a pile and staple them together like a book.

EXTENSIONS

- A group of artists can create one large oil pastel drawing and then paint over it together with liquid watercolors.
- Draw with oil pastels. Then dip a cotton swab in cooking oil and paint the lines and spaces of the drawing. The oil pastels will break down and blend colors.

Laminations

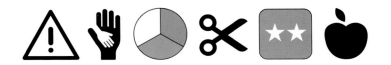

Everyone under the age of 12 must experience laminations at least once, whether in school, childcare, or scout troops. Laminations may have been around as long as waxed paper has existed! Explore laminations again and again. Artists discover and observe how shaved crayon bits interact with heat and waxed paper. Remember to observe caution around heat and electricity.

MATERIALS

| waxed paper | old crayons, crayon stubs | yarn | scissors, optional |
| newspaper | old cheese grater | old iron | hole punch, optional |

PROCESS

1. Place a sheet of waxed paper on a pad of newspaper. The newspaper protects the work surface.
2. With an old cheese grater, grate crayon stubs onto a sheet of waxed paper. Adult help or supervision is needed, depending on the ages of the artists.
3. Cover the shavings with a second sheet of waxed paper. Hint: If this project will hang in a window when complete, insert a piece of yarn between the waxed papers now, letting the loop hang out of the papers.
4. Cover the waxed papers and crayon shavings with more newspaper to absorb any spills or leaks. With a warm iron, quickly press straight down on the covered waxed paper and shavings. Hold the iron in one place while pressing down, then move to another area and press down. Too much heat or too much pressure will muddy the design, so start gently and peek often to see the results. When satisfied with the melting, remove the newspaper.
5. Trim the edges of the lamination if desired, or cut the lamination into any shape. If the yarn is not already sealed into the lamination, use a hole punch to create a hole for yarn to to through. Hang the lamination in the window and let the sun shine through the colors.

Art by child, age 4.
Courtesy Zannifer Rolich, 2021

EXTENSIONS

- Create laminations in small waxed paper sandwich bags for easy beginner laminations.
- Include leaves, yarn, doilies, stickers, cutouts, confetti, sand, glitter, art tissue, or other bits and scraps of things in the lamination before melting.
- Work with dried pressed flowers, dry leaves, or dried seaweed between waxed paper sheets with or without crayon shavings.
- Create a similar project between sheets of clear adhesive contact paper for a no-heat option.

Scribble Cookies

Art by Josephine, age 4.
Courtesy Janine Kloiber, 2021

Old, broken crayons have amazing art properties with spectacular use for all ages. You may find yourself breaking and peeling brand new crayons just because it's so much fun to create these melted crayon disks for coloring, drawing, and making crayon rubbings.

MATERIALS

old crayon stubs, peeled and broken	warm oven
water in a plastic tub or sink	oven mitt
old muffin tin	freezer

Courtesy Janine Kloiber, 2021

PROCESS

1. Save stub ends of old crayons. To remove the paper wrappings easily, soak crayons overnight in water. In the morning most of the crayons will have no paper wrappings.
2. If needed, break the crayon stubs into smaller pieces. Sort colors into an old muffin tin, one color per cup. Or instead, mix colors in each cup to make rainbow-swirled scribble cookies.
3. Place the muffin tin in the warm oven that has been turned off.
4. Keep an eye on the melting crayons, and remove them from the oven when they just turn squishy but are not totally liquid. Use an oven mitt. Adult help is required. (A microwave will not work.)
5. For quickest and easiest removal of scribble cookies, place the muffin tin in the freezer for about a half hour.
6. Remove from the freezer, and the scribble cookies pop right out.

EXTENSIONS

- Kids love metallic colors such as gold, silver, and copper. These colors are available in bulk at school supply stores.
- Assign this muffin tin to crayon and art uses from now on to avoid cleaning the wax from its surface. Muffin tins come in handy for many melted crayon art activities. However, if you must return it to baking use, the muffin tin will wash in very hot soapy water.

Warmed Crayon

Warm, smooth, fragrant melted crayons seem to have a calming effect on even the most active artists. Drawing on a heated electric warming tray allows crayon to melt as the drawing progresses. Artists will discover mixing melted colors. Melted crayon art will appear waxy and translucent. This activity is best accomplished by one artist at a time for safety. Hint: Moving the crayon slowly allows for the best melting.

MATERIALS

electric warming tray, set on low or
   medium-low
aluminum foil
peeled crayons

paper: white copying paper, thin
   paper plates, squares of construction paper
oven mitt, mittens, or work gloves
newspaper for drying

PROCESS

1. Locate a warming tray from a thrift shop, yard sale, or grandparent's kitchen. They are inexpensive and have many uses.
2. Cover the warming tray with foil, if desired. Foil makes cleanup easy but is not required. The warming tray will wipe clean with a rag or paper towel if the tray is still warm. Hint: Wear an oven mitt or work glove on the nondrawing hand to steady the paper on the warming tray. Draw with the free hand.

3. Place a sheet of paper directly on the foil or on the tray, holding it in place with the protected nondrawing hand. Draw on the warmed paper with crayon using the drawing hand. Draw slowly so the crayon can melt easily while drawing.
4. Hang the cooled design in a window or hold up to the light to see the light shine through the wax.
5. Wipe the tray with a rag or towel while it is still warm for the next artist to use.

EXTENSIONS

- Draw directly on the warming tray with or without foil, and no paper. When a melted design is complete, press a sheet of paper against the melted design. Then lift the paper by the corner. A print of the melted design will have transferred to the paper.
- Draw on fabric that has been stretched across and taped to the warming tray.
- Create little designs on folded note paper to make unique greeting cards.

Courtesy Cindi Frakes Zieger, Sunny Days Preschool, 2021

Encaustic Painting

When crayon is melted and softened, the colors can be painted on paper or other background material with a brush. The melted crayon reacts like thick paint. It dries quickly and hardens on the paper, resembling the look of oil painting. As with all art activities involving heat or electricity, closely observe caution and safety.

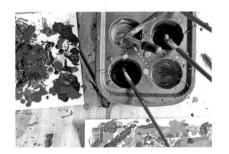

Ana Dziengel, BabbleDabbleDo, 2021

MATERIALS

warming tray or electric frying pan

old paintbrushes

aluminum foil

old muffin tin (not for baking)

crayon stubs, peeled and broken

PROCESS

1. Sort crayon stubs into the cups of an old muffin tin by color. Be sure the paper has been removed. Hint: Soak crayon stubs overnight in a tub of water. Most of the paper will fall off.
2. Cover the warming tray or electric frying pan with aluminum foil to protect the surface from crayon. Secure this heat source carefully to protect the artist. This activity works best with one child at a time. Observe caution. Adult supervision is required.
3. Set the muffin tin on the warming tray with the heat set to low. If low does not melt the crayon, increase heat to a comfortable setting.
4. When the crayon has melted to a squishy liquid state, dip an old paintbrush into the squishy crayon and paint quickly and directly on paper. Mix colors on the paper. The crayon dries quickly on the paper, so keep dipping the brush in the melted crayon to keep it soft and full of color. The completed artwork will dry in a few minutes.

HINTS

- If the crayon cools or hardens in the tin, reheat and melt. The same holds true for the paintbrushes. If the crayon hardens on the brush, dip the brush into warm melted crayon until the wax on the brush melts again.
- The muffin tin and brushes should be assigned to melted crayon work from now on.
- Brace the muffin tin to prevent tipping or spilling. Be sure the cord for the warming tool is out of the way.

EXTENSION

- Paint with melted crayon on rocks, wood, mat board, or other surfaces.

Foldout Art Gallery

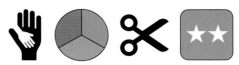

The pages of this art gallery are like a book that folds out in a long, continuous accordion-style display from front to back. It can tell a story, become a bundle of connected ideas, or simply display a collection of process artworks.

MATERIALS

2 pieces of mat board or cardboard squares for the covers,
 8 by 8 inches
mat board or poster board squares for the pages,
 8 by 8 inches
masking tape
crayons, markers
saved artworks that can be cut, optional

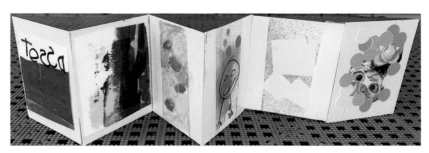

Art by Tessa, age 5.
Courtesy MaryAnn Kohl, 2021

PROCESS

1. Each artist should review their art collection and select pieces that they would like to put in their gallery. The pieces can share a theme or color, or just reflect the artist's feelings that day!
2. Tape the boards together with masking tape so that the pages fold in an accordion style. It helps to leave a small gap between the boards when the tape is applied so the boards will fold out easily. The tape will cover the gap.

3. Tape or glue selected artworks on the drawing boards, one artwork for each board. Artists may wish to attach artworks on both sides of each board. A title or other words may also be written on the covers or on the pages.
4. Fold the gallery into a book shape, or open the gallery zigzag and display it on a table or shelf.

EXTENSIONS

• Draw pictures or designs around a theme or topic.
• Illustrate a favorite story or tale, or one made up by the artist.

Pastel Chalk Smudging

Creating smudged chalk art is an art technique with an "ooh-aah" quality as the smudged chalk lines change before the eyes. Although the directions are somewhat more involved than for many other chalk art activities, the resulting beauty and magic are worth the effort.

MATERIALS

old file folders or lightweight cardboard
scissors
facial tissues or cotton balls

chalk pastels (not sidewalk chalk)
paper (try both dark and light colors)

Courtesy MaryAnn Kohl, 2021

PROCESS

1. Fold a square cut from an old file folder or piece of lightweight cardboard in half. Cut any shape from the fold. Remove the solid shape. Keep both the solid shape and the shape with the hole. Both can be used as stencils with entirely different art results.

Positive Solid Stencil
- Place the solid shape on the paper.
- Trace around the shape with wide, heavy chalk lines while holding the stencil firmly in place with the nondrawing hand.
- Pick up a piece of tissue or a cotton ball in the drawing hand. Brush the chalk outline gently with the tissue or cotton, brushing out and away from the solid shape.
- Remove the stencil. The effect will be soft and muted with a distinct stencil design with clean edges. Repeat as desired.

Negative Hole Stencil
- Repeat the same actions from step 2, this time tracing inside the hole cut from the square.
- Hold the stencil in place and brush the chalk lines inward into the hole.
- Remove the stencil and see the opposite design effect compared to step 2.

EXTENSIONS
- Make repetitive overlapping patterns by moving the stencil slightly with each tracing and smudging.
- Overlap stencils and designs for a mixing of colors and shapes. Experiment with a variety of overlapping colors.
- Find objects to use as stencil templates: soup can, shoe, comb, cup, or other objects.

Wet Paper Chalk

The normal dusty, pale qualities of chalk are upscaled when the chalk particles are absorbed by water, making the chalk brighter and less smudgy. For even brighter chalk drawings, soak the drawing end of the chalk in sugar water for ten minutes, which also reduces smearing.

MATERIALS

drawing paper (not newsprint or copying paper)
colored chalk pastels (not sidewalk chalk)
water in a bowl
sponge

PROCESS

1. Wet a sheet of paper with a damp sponge. Soak up any puddles. The paper should be moist but not dripping.
2. Draw on the damp paper with different colors of chalk.
3. Chalk can also be dipped into the water and used wet.
4. Dry the art completely.

EXTENSIONS

- To further reduce smearing, an adult may spray the chalk drawing outside with a fixative such as hairspray, clear enamel, or polymer craft spray.
- Sponge print: Draw on a wet sponge with chalk and then press the sponge on dry paper. Lift the sponge, and a print will be transferred to the paper.

Courtesy Sunshine and Puddles Family Day Care, 2021

Sidewalk Chalk & Tape

A sidewalk square becomes the perfect canvas for chalk art! With sidewalk chalk, fill sections designated by lines of masking tape. Then brush and blend the chalk further to completely fill the shapes. Pull away the tape and see the stunning design! The art will remain until the next rain washes it away.

MATERIALS

sidewalk square
sidewalk chalk
broom

masking tape
rags or sponges

PROCESS

1. Choose a square section of the sidewalk. Sweep it clean before beginning the art.
2. Pull long strips of masking tape from the roll. Stick them to the sidewalk to form shapes of any kind. Crossing lines of tape over each other is fine. Make many lines or just a few, deciding how the design will form.
3. Begin coloring in the sections formed by the tape. To help the chalk fill in easily, brush the chalk coloring with rags or a slightly damp sponge. Blend and form new colors too!
4. When ready, pull away the tape. The resulting design will be bright and interesting. Perhaps over the next several days it will cheer the folks walking along.
5. The rain will wash away the art so no specific cleanup is needed.

EXTENSIONS

- Each sidewalk square can be an individual canvas for a chalk drawing.
- For brighter chalk colors, moisten the sidewalk squares and then draw with chalk.
- With a broom and water, brush the chalk art until it disappears. Artists often enjoy hard work like cleaning away chalk on a sidewalk.

Art by Graham, age 6, and Avery, age 2.
Courtesy Caitlin Rot, 2021

Painted Chalk

Dipping colored chalk into white tempera paint causes the chalk to take on a new property. The chalk will outline itself in white when drawing on paper. Chalk can also be dipped into other colors. Experiment to see the possibilities.

MATERIALS

colored chalk or chalk pastels
2 tablespoons thick white tempera paint in a jar lid
tempera paint in other colors in lids, optional
black or dark paper
other colors of paper, optional

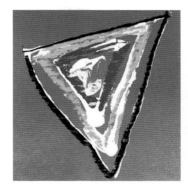
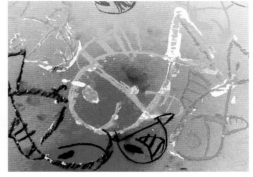

Triangle Design by Parker, age 8   *School of Fish* by Parker, age 8

PROCESS

1. Dip the end of a piece of colored chalk into thick white tempera in a shallow jar lid.
2. Draw with the whitened, moist chalk. The marks will distinctly show the color of the chalk edged with white against dark paper.
3. Experiment with other colors of tempera paint and other colors of background papers.

EXTENSIONS

- Experiment with dipping the chalk in black paint and then drawing on white paper.
- Create a sampler of strokes and markings as an experiment in lines:
  - zigzags
  - spirals
  - dots
  - straight lines
  - curves
  - letters

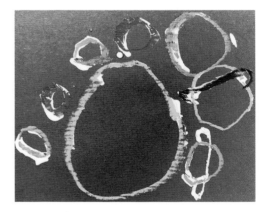

The Solar System by Lucas, age 5

- Draw with chalk on paper. Cover another paper with white tempera paint. Then press the chalk drawing face down into the wet, white-painted paper. Lift off the drawing and see the print.

Shadow Chalk

Art by child, age 5.
Courtesy Karen Begley,
www.natureplaystudios.com, 2021

Join with a friend on a sunny day and head outside to create a shadow artwork with sidewalk chalk. One friend poses in a way that their shadow falls clearly on a sidewalk or playground. While the posing friend holds still, the artist friend traces the shadow shape. Then both friends color in and decorate the shadow shape with chalk together. No friends handy? Create a shadow chalk design from a bicycle, a tree, flowers, or any objects making shadows.

MATERIALS

sunny day
sidewalk chalk
sidewalk or playground
2 children, optimal
rags for blending chalk, optional

PROCESS

1. One friend poses so their shadow falls clearly on a sidewalk or playground. The other friend traces the shapes of the shadow with sidewalk chalk.
2. Both friends work together to color in and decorate the shadow shape. Rags are handy for blending and smoothing chalk, helping to fill in the shape.
3. Rain will eventually wash away the chalk art, so cleanup is easy.

EXTENSIONS

- Search for shadows on the sidewalk or playground. A bicycle, flower, or tree will make a great shadow. Trace, color, and blend with sidewalk chalk as above.
- Look for shadows indoors. Trace with crayons and color in and decorate the shadow shape on a sheet of paper.

Art by child, age 7.
Courtesy Karen Begley,
www.natureplaystudios.com, 2021

Crushed Chalk

Painting with chalk is an inspiring art technique accomplished by crushing chalk sticks to powder and then using a wet paintbrush to apply the powder to paper. The beauty of the chalk powder is that the colors will mix and blend during the painting. Crushed bright chalk pastels offers the brightest colors, whereas other colored chalk will be paler.

MATERIALS

colored chalk
rock
waxed paper or paper plate
muffin tin or other small containers
    to hold crushed chalk powder

water in dish
paintbrushes
paper

Art by Callahan, age 2.
Courtesy Brittany Dusek, 2021

PROCESS

1. Crush a stick of colored pastel chalk or other chalk with a rock on a paper plate or waxed paper. Do not pound the chalk. Press the rock gently but firmly against the chalk, rocking it a little until it crushes the chalk to powder.
2. Slip the powdered chalk into a small container such as the cups of a muffin tin.
3. Now crush more colors and prepare more cups of powder.
4. When there are multiple colors ready, dip a small paintbrush into water, and then dip it into the powdered chalk.
5. Then apply the wet powdered chalk to paper. This is painting with chalk!

Art by Josephine, age 4, and Leonard, age 6.
Courtesy Janine Kloiber, 2021

EXTENSIONS

- Dip a paintbrush into liquid starch and then into crushed chalk. Paint on paper.
- Paint with small pieces of wet sponge dipped in crushed chalk.
- Dip a finger in water and then in crushed chalk. Draw with the chalky finger.
- Experiment mixing different colors of crushed chalk in a single muffin-tin cup, rather than just one color in a cup.

Sponge Chalk Print

Chalk has always been a favorite medium for young artists. Making a chalk print is easy and effective. Draw with chalk on a flat, wet sponge, and then press the sponge drawing on paper. A chalk print will transfer to the paper. Artists can also dip a wet sponge into crushed chalk and press it on paper to make a sponge print or drawing.

MATERIALS

flat sponges
water in a pan or bowl
colored chalk (pastel chalk works better than sidewalk chalk)
paper
towels to dry hands

(above and right)
Art by Declan Benner, age 6.
Courtesy Brittany Dusek, 2021

PROCESS

1. Dip a flat sponge in a pan or bowl of water and wring it out. Dry hands if necessary.
2. Draw with chalk on the flat wet sponge.
3. Press the sponge onto a piece of paper to make a chalk print. Several prints could be possible from one drawing.
4. Redraw over the same design on the sponge to make the same print over and over. Or, rinse the sponge and make a new drawing.

EXTENSIONS

- Color little pieces of wet sponge with chalk and make chalk print dots.
- Crush chalk into powder and dip a wet sponge into the powder. Brush the chalky sponge on paper like painting.
- Experiment with different colors of paper. Black or dark blue paper can be effective with bright chalk colors.

Art by Emma Dusek, age 1.

3

Paint & Dye

Experi-Paint

Many different materials and tools can be used to paint with, and just as many materials can be painted on. The challenge and experience of "experi-painting" is trying many combinations without concern as to how the art project will turn out. The success of experi-painting is in the process and experimentation, not the final product.

MATERIALS

TYPES OF PAINT	PAINT TOOLS	PAINT SURFACES	MIX WITH PAINT	PAPER TYPES
acrylic paint	broom	branch	coffee grounds	absorbent
bold and heavy paint	bubbles	brick	corn syrup	bumpy
dry paints on wet paper	clay	cardboard	cornstarch	crumpled
food coloring	corncob	cookie sheet	egg shells	folded
glossy paint	cotton ball	craft sticks	eggs	fuzzy
light or delicate paint	cotton swab	fabric	flour	glazed
liquid tempera paint	craft sticks	foil	flower petals	rolled
liquid watercolors	duster	ice	glitter	scored
mud paint	feathers	leaf	glue	smooth
powdered tempera	hands and feet	mirror	Jell-O	sticky
salty paint	gadgets	paper	Kool-Aid	textured
thick or thin paint	kitchen utensils	plexiglass	liquid starch	torn
watercolor paint box	leaf	poster	milk	transparent
wet paint on wet paper	sponge	rock	rain	with holes
whipped paint	spray bottle	snow	salt	wrinkled
	sticks	table	sand	
	string, yarn	tile	sawdust	
	toys	tray		
		wall		
		window		
		wood scraps		

Art by child, age 4.
Courtesy Mary Turner, Mimi's House Family Childcare, 2021

Art by Valerie Thompson, age 4.
Courtesy Trisha Thompson, 2021

PROCESS

1. Experiment with techniques, tools, and surfaces.
2. Experiment, create, explore.
3. Recycle or save paint experiments.
4. Let the imagination soar with painting.

Art by Isabelle, age 1.
Courtesy Mary Turner, Mimi's House Family Childcare, 2021

Damp Paper Paint

Painting on damp paper causes the water to thin the paint, producing a soft, blurred, blended effect. The painting experience itself has a gentle, calm quality. Use a soft touch and observe the paints flowing and blurring with the water.

MATERIALS

flat pan or baking pan
good drawing paper or
    butcher paper, cut to fit

paper towels
paints: watercolor, tempera,
    or food coloring

paintbrushes
jars of water
newspaper

PROCESS

1. Fill a flat pan with water. Place the sheet of paper in the pan to moisten. Remove.
2. Place the paper on a table while still wet.
3. Use a paper towel to blot off some excess moisture, but keep the paper shiny and wet.
4. Paint on the wet paper. Experiment with dripping, swirling, blending, and mixing colors on the paper. Dip the paintbrush in the jar of water when changing colors to clean the brush. Or let the colors mix.
5. Leave the art on the table to dry, or place the painting on a dry sheet of newspaper and carry to a drying area.

Art by Elli Harney, age 7.
Courtesy Megan Harney, ourhandcraftedlife.com, 2021

EXTENSIONS

- Ways to moisten paper:
  - wash over the paper with a big brush full of water
  - fill a sponge with water and dampen paper
  - hold the paper under the faucet
- Experiment with a variety of papers, such as:
  - paper grocery bag
  - textured paper
  - construction paper
  - watercolor paper

- For a batik effect, crumple the wet paper and then spread it out on a table. Paint on the paper as usual. When dry, the crackled look of batik will result.

Art by child, age 2.
Courtesy Natalie Valentine

Marking Pen Paint

Painting with water over the marks made from water-based marking pens is similar to techniques used in "paint with water" books found near coloring book shelves in some stores. In this art experience, the picture or design is created by the individual young artist's imagination and not by a commercial illustrator.

MATERIALS

water-based markers or pens
smooth, heavy paper:
 drawing paper
 finger paint paper
 tagboard
 poster board

water
soft paintbrushes, 1 fine and 1 broad
misting bottle filled with water, optional

PROCESS

1. Draw with a water-based marker on paper.
2. While the marker lines are fresh, dip a paintbrush in water. Paint over the fresh marker lines and shapes. New markers allow for better painting than overly dry ones. The water will blur the marker lines.
3. Use the wet paintbrush frequently. No need to finish the drawing first. Paint along while drawing. If you have a misting bottle, you can spray the marker lines to blur marker lines quickly and completely.
4. When the drawing or design is finished, let it dry. Some artists like to paint the finished dry drawing with watercolors to add more color and design.

EXTENSIONS

- Draw with water-based markers on wet paper.
- Draw around stencil shapes and designs with markers, and then paint the lines with water.

Art by Exra, age 3½.
Courtesy Emma Koehler

Spattered Stencils

Young artists tend to enjoy spattering paint! This stencil version is more focused and best done outdoors. Friends and bare feet add to the fun. Large paper, paintbrushes, and cups of tempera paint combine for discovery and exploration creating stencil designs. Add some music for inspiration!

MATERIALS

old file folders
scissors
rocks to weight paper corners
drawing tool, optional (crayon, pencil, marker)

tempera paints, in
   handheld cups
paintbrushes
large paper

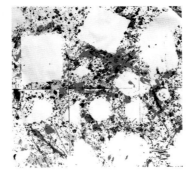

Art by Miles LaMothe, age 10.
Courtesy Carey LaMothe

Art by Emerson Jackson, age 5.
Courtesy Christine Kellerman, Anderson Prep Preschool, 2021

PROCESS

1. Cut shapes from old file folders. These will be the stencils. Big shapes are encouraged! Stars, circles, hearts, clouds, letters, or any individually designed stencil shapes are all possible. The stencil can first be drawn and then cut, or can be cut freehand.
2. Spread the large paper on the grass. Too windy? Weight the corners with rocks to keep it from blowing away.
3. Place shapes in any fashion or design on the paper. Too windy? Place a small rock on each shape to hold in place.
4. Dip the paintbrush into tempera paint, and then shake and drip colorful drops on the paper and over the stencils. Continue changing colors and exploring ways to get great spatters. Don't be surprised to see spatters on feet, clothes, hands, or faces.
5. When complete, let the painting dry briefly. Then remove the stencil shapes. Observe the stencil shapes that remain white amid all the color.

Art by Lucas Driver, age 4.
Courtesy Christine Kellerman, Anderson Prep Preschool, 2021

EXTENSIONS

- Display the completed spattered stencil as a banner or poster on a wall. Announce an event or share a message painted over the stencil design.
- Create stencil spatters on an old white sheet instead of paper.

Salt Painting

Courtesy Cindi Frakes Zieger, Sunny Days Preschool, 2021

Mix several cups of salt paint in different colors for a rainbow of crystal colors. The salt mixture creates a crystallized painting as the artwork dries.

MATERIALS

liquid starch
water
tempera paint, liquid watercolors, or food coloring
table salt
cups for mixing the salt-paint solution
paper plate, mat board, or cardboard
paintbrushes

PROCESS

1. Mix the following in a cup:
   ⅛ cup liquid starch
   ⅛ cup water
   1 tablespoon tempera paint or liquid watercolors, or 2 squirts food coloring
   ½ cup table salt
2. Mix several cups of the mixture, each with a different color.
3. Apply the mixture to the paper or board with a paintbrush. Stir the mixture often while painting.
4. The painting will crystallize as it dries.

EXTENSIONS

- Salt painting is especially effective for winter and snow designs.
- Mix Epsom salts or rock salt into the paint to see crystals that are shaped differently than table salt.

Salty Watercolor

Many young (and not so young) artists say they like salty watercolor the best of all the art experiences in this book. There is something magical about the way the watercolors gently touch the salt and travel through the design on their own. Mystifying and delightful! Use lots of watery paint and a gentle quick touch with the brush.

MATERIALS

white glue in a squeeze bottle
base material: mat board, heavy paper plate, or cardboard
plastic tub big enough for the base to lay flat
2–3 cups of salt
liquid watercolors in shallow cups or a watercolor paint box
small paintbrush with a good point
jar of water for rinsing

Courtesy Cindi Frakes-Zieger, Sunny Days Preschool, 2021

Art by Graham, age 6, and Avery, age 2.
Courtesy Caitlin Rot, 2021

PROCESS

1. Draw a thick design with white glue on mat board or other heavy backing. Use a good amount of glue and thick lines.
2. Fill the bottom of the flat tub with salt. Place the glue drawing in the tub and use hands to scoop salt over the entire drawing.
3. Lift and tilt the design while still in the tub so that the salt falls back into the tub.
4. Return to the table with the glue-and-salt design.
5. Fill a paintbrush with paint. The paint works best if it is runny, so feel free to soak the brush in water and then dip in paint.

6. Gently touch the tip of the soaking brush to the salt and let the paint absorb into the salt and travel into the design. Try not to paint or scrub with the paintbrush into the glue and salt. Only light touches are needed.
7. Rinse the brush as you go.
8. Dry completely. Be aware that the salt can crack and fall off the backing, so consider slipping it in a plastic bag or wrapping it with clear plastic wrap and a little tape. Otherwise, try not to bend the backing to help prevent the salt from cracking.

Art by Graham, age 6.
Courtesy Caitlin Rot, 2021

Multi-Fun Paints

So many recipes for paint in combination with another ingredient are possible! Many favorites are listed, but always know you can invent your own. Each ingredient adds a new dimension to the properties of tempera paint. All require little or no extra expense and can actually extend the life and quantity of tempera paint over time. Keep in mind that this activity and the recipes are discovery experiments. Results will vary.

Art by child, age 4.
*Courtesy Jennifer Goodman Crowell,
the Child Development Cooperative,
Baton Rouge, LA*

MATERIALS

tempera paint

bowls or cups for mixing paint

painting tools: paintbrushes, craft sticks, spoons

jar of water for rinsing

paper, cardboard, or other base

List of Ingredients to Explore:

Mix liquid or powdered tempera paint to any desired consistency with one of the following ingredients. (Stir in a little water if the paint seems too thick.)

baby oil—will not dry (no water)
corn syrup—glossy, sticky (no water)
cornstarch—porcelain quality
egg yolk—bright, sticky, glossy
liquid starch—smooth, translucent
paste—thick, textured, frosting-like

shampoo—whip until fluffy
shaving cream—squeeze or drop paint on, swirl in with a small brush
sweetened condensed milk—glazed, shiny
whipped soap flakes—thick, billowy
white glue—shiny

PROCESS

1. Mix tempera paint, liquid or powdered, with one of the ingredients in the list above. For example, pour white glue into a cup and add tempera paint, stirring with a paintbrush. A little water may be added to thin very thick paint.
2. Paint as with any paint on paper. For very thick paint recipes, spread the paint like frosting with a craft stick or spoon as if using a palette knife. Experiment with squeezing the paint from a bottle or cake decorating bag.
3. Dry the artwork completely.
4. Continue experimenting with new ideas of mixtures and combinations.

*Courtesy Jennifer Goodman Crowell,
the Child Development Cooperative,
Baton Rouge, LA*

Watercolor Paints & Pen

Bring out the bright liquid watercolors for a two-step painting experience. All you need is paint, paper, paintbrush, and a permanent marker.

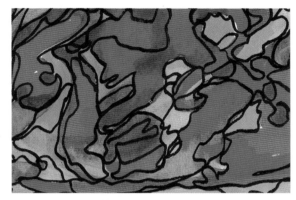
Courtesy MaryAnn Kohl, 2021

MATERIALS

plastic or newspaper, optional
shallow cups or muffin tin
liquid watercolors
paintbrushes
jar of water for rinsing
paper
black permanent marker, such as Sharpie (other colors optional)

PROCESS

1. Protect the worktable with plastic or newspaper if needed.
2. Pour liquid watercolors into shallow cups or a muffin tin. Use at least three colors.
3. Paint the entire sheet of paper, filling the paper with colors. Leaving some unpainted is fine, but try to paint out and over the edges.
4. Allow the painting to dry, which won't take long. Liquid watercolors dry quickly.
5. When dry, look at the painting and see where colors meet and blend or shapes are made.
6. With the black marker, chose to trace and outline whatever lines or shapes seem interesting or appealing.

EXTENSIONS

- Painting on watercolor paper will produce an absorbent, blended look.
- Experiment using markers other than black.

Art by Graham, age 6.
Courtesy Caitlin Rot, 2021

Plastic Wrap Roll Painting

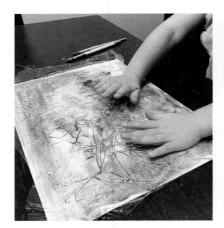 

(above and right) Courtesy Heather Ann Goodman, Cascade View Christian School, 2021

Everyone loves to be surprised, and rolling over a fresh, wet painting covered with plastic wrap will definitely offer just that! A rolling pin will spread the paint under the plastic in a most surprising way.

MATERIALS

craft canvas or heavy drawing paper
masking tape, optional
tempera or acrylic paints in shallow cups
paintbrushes
clear plastic wrap
rolling pin

PROCESS

1. Place the paper or craft canvas on the work space. Some artists like to tape the corners with masking tape to help keep the paper or canvas steady, preventing wiggling or slipping.
2. Paint with thick lines and shapes of paint. Cover the canvas or paper in any way, but don't let it dry out. Work fairly quickly.
3. Pull a sheet of plastic wrap from its roll and spread it over the painting. Pat it in place by hand so it sticks to the paint.
4. Roll over the plastic wrap with a rolling pin. Roll up and down, left and right, rolling in all directions.
5. When ready, peel the plastic wrap carefully from the painting. See how the original painting has changed!

EXTENSIONS

- Follow the steps above, but instead of a rolling pin, use fingers and hands like finger painting to move and push the paint about.
- Place some cut-out paper shapes on heavy drawing paper. Then drop blobs of paint around and over them. Cover with plastic wrap. Roll over the painting with a rolling pin. Remove the plastic wrap and remove the paper shapes at the end.

Art by Kelsey, age 4.
Courtesy Kelly Hinds, Stock School, Chicago, IL, 2021

Puff-It Paint

Thin paint is transformed into unique designs when the artist blows through a straw and directs the paint into fanlike patterns. Blow gently to begin with, and then experiment with different strengths of air and tilting of the straw.

MATERIALS

paper
tray with sides, optional
paints in any color, poured into shallow cups:
    thinned tempera paint
    liquid watercolors
    food coloring mixed with a little water

paintbrush or spoon, one for each color
drinking straws

PROCESS

1. Place the paper on the table or in a tray with sides.
2. Spoon or brush a little puddle of paint or food coloring on the paper.
3. Point a straw in the direction the paint will go and place the straw to the lips. Blow air out. The paint will spread out like a fan and make patterns and designs.
4. Add more colors. Continue blowing and creating designs. Colors may cross over one another, making new colors and shapes.
5. Remove the art to a drying area. Then repeat with a new sheet of paper.
6. Allow the art to dry completely.

EXTENSIONS

- Blow paint puddles with other tools like a turkey baster or a hair blow-dryer.
- Use black paint on white paper to make black-and-white designs.
- Sprinkle dots of paint on the paper. Blow clear water through the paint.
- Blow puddles of paint on a cookie sheet. Press a sheet of paper on the paint and lift a print.

Art by child, age 4.
Courtesy Zannifer Rolich, 2021

Pulled String

Place paint-soaked string between a folded sheet of paper, press down with one hand, then pull the string out with the other hand. Intriguing designs and mixtures of colors happen quickly. Sometimes younger artists need help controlling the string and paper, but results are always impressive.

MATERIALS

white or colored paper, folded in half
2 or more colors of tempera paint on a plate or tray or in bowls
yarn or string in 1-foot lengths (manageable length for most ages)
paper towels or wet sponge for wiping hands

PROCESS

1. Open a prefolded sheet of paper and place it on the table beside the containers of paint.
2. Hold one end of the yarn and drop the rest of the yarn into the paint, keeping hold of the dry end. Swirl it around to coat it well.
3. Lift the yarn out of the paint and place it on one-half of the opened sheet of paper. Some artists like to curl it this way and that, while others let it fall as it may. Hint: It helps to keep the dry end of the string hanging off the edge of the paper.
4. Fold the paper over the paint-soaked string. Use the free hand to do the folding.
5. Press down on the paper with the free hand. Pressing down and holding firm, pull the yarn out with the other hand. Set the yarn aside. Open the paper and look at the design.
6. Repeat the steps above with a new color and a separate yarn strand. Use a separate strand for each color.
7. When satisfied with the paint design, dry completely with the paper open.

EXTENSIONS

- Experiment using thick or thin paint.
- Experiment using thick or thin string, ribbon, or a variety of yarns.
- Cut out the designs when dry.

Courtesy Heather Ann Goodman, Cascade View Christian School, 2021

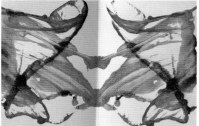

Art by child, age 5.
Courtesy Zannifer Rolich, 2021

Blottos

Young artists can learn about symmetry by dotting paint onto paper and then folding two sides together. When opened again, the artist will discover a unique mix of interesting shapes and colors. Shapes often resemble butterflies, monsters, or flowers because of the symmetry, but a predetermined design is not expected. Enjoy the surprise of color and design!

MATERIALS

construction paper, in colors, or other paper of choice
tempera paint in cups, several colors
spoon or paintbrush for each cup

PROCESS

1. Fold the paper in half. Open it. Place it on the work space.
2. Spoon or brush drops and blobs of paint on the fold and on one side of the paper.
3. Refold the paper.
4. With the palm of the hand, press and rub the paper from the fold out to the edge of the paper.
5. Open the paper and observe the design.
6. More color can be added and the steps repeated. Some artists will work at the skill of creating planned designs through experimentation, while others will continue to delight in the surprise paint designs that are made.
7. Set the art aside to dry and create more blottos.

EXTENSIONS

- When the blotto is dry, cut out the design. Glue onto a contrasting color of paper.
- Create butterflies, flowers, bugs, or creatures. Add other characteristics with markers.
- Read the book *It Looked Like Spilt Milk* (Charles Green Shaw) or *Little Cloud* (Eric Carle) for ideas about what blotto shapes can look like to different people. Then create white blottos on blue paper.

Courtesy MaryAnn Kohl, 2021

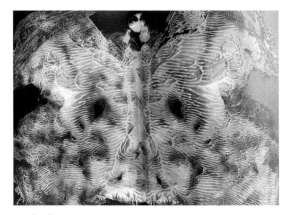

Art by Raegan, age 4.
Courtesy Amy Kay, 2021

Squeezing Paint

Art by children, age 2.
Courtesy Jennifer Goodman Crowell, the Child Development Cooperative, Baton Rouge, LA

Art by child, age 3.
Courtesy Zannifer Rolich, 2021

Any time a new way of painting is explored, the understanding of what paint and paint tools are capable of accomplishing expands to new heights! The effects of squeezing paint are completely different than using a paintbrush, and the practice opens many new possibilities for creativity.

MATERIALS

squeeze container: picnic ketchup or mustard bottle, shampoo or conditioner bottle, dish detergent bottle, squirt toys
tempera paints
sheets of paper, medium or large size

PROCESS

1. Fill empty squeeze containers with tempera paints.
2. Spread the paper on the floor or on the grass.
3. Squeeze the paint out onto the paper. Use gentle pressure.
4. Move the opening of the container about, drawing or making designs.
5. Dry the painting or design completely.

EXTENSIONS

- Squeezing color is effective on a very large surface or even on a vertical surface such as a wall or a fence. Prepare for dripping and excitement. Remember gentle squeezing works the best.
- Add other painting tools to explore:
  - balloons
  - brushes
  - cotton balls
  - cotton swabs
  - hands and feet
  - plastic knife
  - sponges
  - spoons
  - sticks
  - straws
  - turkey baster

Puffy Paint Dough

Flour, water, salt, and paint combine to make a squeezable dough with the best qualities of both paint and dough. When the colors are squeezed on paper, they will not mix even when they pool together. The mixture then hardens into a puffy shape, with a glistening quality caused by the salt crystals.

MATERIALS

equal parts of flour, salt, and water (start with 1 cup of each)
spoon and bowl for each color
tempera paints or liquid watercolors
empty plastic squeeze bottles or containers:
    condiment bottle
    shampoo bottle
    frosting decorating tool
cardboard squares, mat board, paper plates, poster board

Art by Madeline, age 4.
Courtesy Christine Kellerman, Anderson Prep Preschool, 2021

PROCESS

1. Measure and mix equal parts of flour, salt, and water in a bowl. Prepare separate bowls for each color. One cup of each ingredient per paint color is a good start.
2. Add paint to each bowl to create color in the desired amount. For pastel colors, add a little paint. For bright colors, add more paint.
3. Pour or spoon the mixture into the empty squeeze bottles. Bottles with wider openings are the easiest to fill.
4. Gently squeeze the mixture onto the paper, making designs or drawings. Experiment with different colors touching each other. Notice how the colors do not mix but simply pool close together.
5. Continue repeating and creating with the puffy paint dough. The art will dry hard, crystallized and shiny.
6. The mixture will store in a covered container in the refrigerator for a day or two but will eventually dry out. Washing out containers is much easier when the mixture is still fresh and moist.

Courtesy Cindi Frakes Zieger, Sunny Days Preschool, 2021

Toy Tracks

Art by Jaden Reuben, age 4.
Courtesy Jansi Rani R, www.instagram.com /craftish_mom, 2021

Art by child, age 4.
Courtesy Cristy Ward, 2021

If an art room has a reluctant artist, this activity will invite and involve even the most skeptical individual. Driving wheeled toys through paint and then across large sheets of paper is not only beautiful but also great fun. Explore the toy box for different types of wheeled toys.

MATERIALS

liquid starch, optional
cookie sheet or tray with sides
liquid tempera paint
paintbrush for mixing

small toy cars or other wheeled toys
wind-up hopping and walking toys
large sheet of paper

PROCESS

1. Pour a puddle of liquid starch onto the cookie sheet or tray. If you don't have starch, skip this step. Any thinned paint will work fine.
2. Squeeze a big spoonful of paint into the starch puddle. Mix the paint and starch together with a paintbrush.
3. Roll a small toy car through the paint mixture. Then drive the car across a piece of paper, creating tracks. Drive around until the paint fades.
4. Redip the wheels and roll again.
5. Choose another wheeled toy and roll it through the paint and then over the paper.
6. Cleanup: It's best to relegate these toys to the art center from now on. Simply rinse and air-dry. If this isn't possible, toys can be washed with soap and water and then left to air-dry, before returning to the toy box.

EXTENSIONS

- Place several different colors of paint on the tray so a mixing of colors will occur both on the tray and on the paper.
- Incline a board, cover the board with paper, and then place blobs of paint on the paper. Roll cars, balls, or other objects through the paint down the incline. Have paper at the bottom to catch drips and toys.

Art by Aiden, age 4.
Courtesy Tricia L. Cameron, 2021

Rolling Spheres

Rolling a marble or other round object through paint creates patterns and tracks that are intriguing to create. The shape of the container can also contribute to the possibilities of design, so collect a variety of containers and round objects and see what happens.

MATERIALS

paper or paper plates
scissor, optional
tempera paints in cups
spoons for each cup
bowl of water
paper towels

Containers:
round cakepan
baking pan
shoebox
plastic tray with sides
plastic wading pool
coffee can with lid

Rolling objects:
marbles
golf balls
nerf balls
playground balls
soccer balls or basketballs
orange, cantaloupe, apple

Art by children, ages 2 to 6.
Courtesy Brittany Dusek, 2021

PROCESS

Explore this activity first with marbles. Other rolling spheres can be explored next.

1. Cut paper to fit a round cake pan. A paper plate usually fits nicely.
2. Place a marble in each cup of paint. Spoon out a marble from one of the paint cups and place on the paper in the pan.
3. Tilt the pan, rolling the marble around. Tilt another direction and keep the marble going. Artists will discover tracks and trails of paint from the marble until the paint is used up.

4. Get ready to start again. This time, add multiple marbles on a fresh paper plate in the pan. Tilt the tip the pan to get the marbles rolling and painting. Observe the tracks. Repeat until the design is complete.
5. When ready, remove the marbles with a spoon and plunk them in a bowl of water to rinse. Swirl them around to remove the paint. Dry with paper towels.
6. Remove the paper from the pan and dry.

EXTENSION

- Drop spoonfuls of paints on the paper in the pan and then plop in one marble. Tilt and turn the pan so the marble rolls through the puddles of paint, making designs as it rolls. The shape of the container will contribute to the type of design that occurs. Try round, square, large, and small containers.

Art by child, age 6.
Courtesy Brittany Dusek, 2021

Classic Finger Painting

Art by child, age 4.
Courtesy Ronda Harbaugh, 2021

Art by Otto D'Alton,
age 11 months.
Courtesy Kylie D'Alton, 2021

Finger painting is a classic and basic sensory experience for children. They experience the feel of cool paint moving and sliding about on the paper and between their fingers. They see the direct results of what their fingers and hands can do before their eyes. Two of the best homemade recipes are listed below. The first recipe is the easiest. The second is a cooked finger paint that is smooth and can be painted with while still warm.

MATERIALS

recipe materials, listed below
finger painting paper or paper alternatives: butcher
    paper, poster board, cookie sheet, plastic tray,
    aluminum foil, tabletop
apron or clothing cover

masking tape, optional
newsprint
bucket of soapy water
old towel or paper towels

Recipe 1: Easy Starch Finger Paint

Pour a puddle of liquid starch on the paper. Pour another smaller puddle of tempera paint in the starch puddle. Mix and blend the starch and paint with hands directly on the chosen painting surface.

Recipe 2: Warm Cornstarch Finger Paint

Boil 3 parts (3 cups) water in a pan and remove from the heat. Dissolve 1 part (1 cup) cornstarch in a little cold water. Add to the hot water, stirring constantly.

Return the pan to the heat. Boil the mixture until clear and thick, about one minute. Add food coloring or paint to the mixture. Cool slightly or refrigerate before using.

PROCESS

1. Choose and prepare a finger paint recipe. Prepare the artist and the table for finger painting by covering each appropriately.
2. Spread an open sheet of newsprint on the worktable or floor. Then place the finger paint paper directly on the newsprint. Hint: Taping the corners of the paper can help prevent slipping.
3. Finger painting time! Paint, smear, and blend with hands and fingers. Fingernails can scratch, making finer lines. Ready for arms or elbows? Other tools may be added to the finger painting such as sticks, toothpicks, cotton balls, plastic gift cards, and forks.
4. When the painting experience is complete, the artist should head to the sink or a bucket of soapy water and wash hands. Have an old towel or paper towels on hand. Help may be needed removing the apron. Carry the newsprint with the painting on it to a drying area or dry in place.

Dip & Dye

Oohs and aahs consistently accompany the process of dipping absorbent paper into cups of bright liquid watercolors. Fold coffee filters in any fashion or style and dip a small section or corner into the paint (which we now call the dye). See how the colors spread through the paper and create new colors? When the coffee filters are dry, the resulting colors have changed even more and blended into new shades and hues.

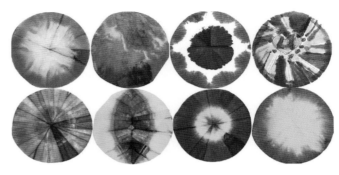

Art by children, ages 6 and 7.
Courtesy Carrie Bryant, Glengarry Elementary School, Nashville, TN, 2021

MATERIALS

liquid watercolors, food coloring, or concentrated food coloring paste
small bowls
newsprint or old towels
coffee filters

PROCESS

1. Pour liquid watercolors into shallow bowls. If using food coloring or concentrated food coloring paste, mix with a small amount of water in each bowl and stir to mix.
2. Spread newsprint or old towels on the work space.
3. Flatten a coffee filter on the work space. Then fold it in any manner.
4. Dip a small corner or edge of the folded coffee filter in a dish of color. Remove quickly. Observe how rapidly the color is absorbed. Then continue to dip into different colors. Oversoaking the coffee filter is common for beginning artists. Controlled dips work best.
5. The coffee filter can be unfolded while wet, but it's also OK to wait until the filter is dry and then unfold.
6. Place the coffee filter on newsprint to dry. Continue dipping and dyeing!

EXTENSIONS

- Spread a coffee filter out on newsprint and dab color on it with a cotton swab, paintbrush, or eyedropper filled with colored water or liquid watercolors.
- Fold and dip other absorbent papers: paper towels, napkins, white wrapping tissue. Dry about halfway, and then unfold carefully.
- Dip and dye a sheet of white wrapping tissue. Dyed tissue makes great wrapping paper for a nice gift when folded, stacked, and tied with a ribbon.
- Wrap a pipe cleaner around the center of a bunched-up coffee filter to make a flower on a stem.

Felt Painting

Dropping liquid watercolors from an eyedropper on a square of felt offers surprising mixes and blends of colors. There is another possibility of discovery: pull colors back into the eyedropper and then redrop the liquid watercolors on the felt again. Discovery, experimentation, and exploration are key in felt painting.

MATERIALS

protective covering for the work area

liquid watercolors in shallow containers (cups, muffin tin, jar lids)

squares of felt (craft or sewing stores have many inexpensive colors)

eyedroppers or pipettes

paintbrushes, optional

jar of water, optional

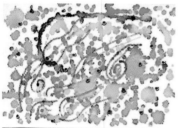

PROCESS

1. Protect the table with newspaper or other covering. Felt tends to absorb color all the way through and onto the work area.
2. Pour liquid watercolors into small cups or other shallow containers on the work space.
3. Place a square of felt on the work space next to the cups of paint.
4. With the eyedropper tip just barely dipping into the paint, squeeze and fill the eyedropper. Then squeeze the color out onto the felt. Observe how the felt absorbs color. A paintbrush can also be used to drop color onto the felt. (If using a brush, rinse the brush often to keep colors bright.) Then add more colors, observing how colors mix and blend.
5. An extra step to try: Remove color from the felt by squeezing the empty eyedropper while directly touching the paint, and pull or suck the paint back into the eyedropper. This paint can be resqueezed and dropped anywhere on the felt.
6. Continue filling the felt with liquid watercolors.
7. When done, dry the felt overnight. If you wish, the felt can be hand-washed to remove most of the color and used again when wet or dry.

Art by children, ages 5 and 8.
Courtesy Larissa Halfond, 2021

EXTENSION

- Other absorbent materials to try: thick paper towels, thick paper napkins, coffee filters, cotton or wool fabric scraps

Grid Painting

Painting within the spaces of a wire grid is an inspiring activity for an individual or a group. Common grids are found from wire shelving, drying racks, wire refrigerator shelves, and even oven racks. Check a thrift store or yard sale for recycled possibilities of racks with sectioned wire areas.

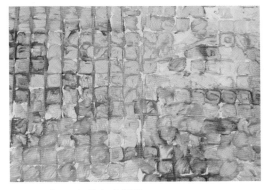

Courtesy Demaris Weitzel, 2021

MATERIALS

poster board, butcher paper, or
   other large paper
wire grid

tempera paints in cups
paintbrushes

PROCESS

1. The floor or a table are ideal work spaces for Grid Painting. Protect the work space with your favorite covering.
2. Place the paper or poster board on the work area.
3. Set a wire rack over the paper.
4. Paint inside each square of the grid with tempera paints. Paint freestyle with all the colors available. Fill in all the squares. Some artists like to use only one color per square, while other artists prefer to mix colors.
5. When the art is complete, remove the wire grid. (Rinse the grid clean when time allows.)
6. When dry, the grid art can be displayed on a wall. Another idea is to place the grid over the same dry grid painting and use new or different colors, painting again.

EXTENSION

Use specific colors to celebrate a theme:
   – red, white, blue—USA, patriotic days
   – red, green, gold—Christmas
   – blue and silver—Hanukkah
   – green, blue, white—Earth Day

Art by Lily Rodriquez and Lolita Arevalo, age 3.
Courtesy Demaris Weitzel, 2021

Palette Painting

Painting with a palette knife allows artists to experiment with thick painting strokes and to see colors mix. First explorations may look a little muddy, but further experiences will yield more focused intentions.

MATERIALS

thick finger paints in muffin tin or cups

any of the following palette painting tools: palette knife, craft stick, plastic knife, tongue depressor

base material: cardboard, poster board, mat board, thick paper

PROCESS

1. Decide to work at a table or an easel. If working at an easel, the artist can hold the muffin tin with paints in the nondrawing hand. Otherwise, set paint cups in the easel tray or on the table.
2. Using a palette knife or similar tool, spread paint on the cardboard like you would spread frosting on a cake. Push the paint about, making designs in the thick paint.
3. Add more paint colors and mix the colors directly on the cardboard. Experiment with the end, sides, and point of the palette knife or tool.
4. The painting will need overnight drying or longer due to the thickness of the paint.

Art by Evie, age 2.
Courtesy Megan Collins, 2021

How to Thicken Tempera Paint

Add 4 level teaspoons of cornstarch to 3 cups of water in a pot, mixing until all combined. Heat the mixture over low heat, stirring until the cornstarch dissolves and is smooth and thick. Then cool. Slowly pour the thickener into each color or container of tempera paint, stirring until the thickness desired is reached. Keep the remaining thickener in a refrigerated sealed container. Stir before using again.

EXTENSIONS

- Explore additional tools for spreading, mixing, and painting: cotton swab, stick, spatula, spoon, paintbrush handle.
- Place blobs of paint on a plastic plate. The artist stands at the easel and uses one brush to mix shades and tints of paint on the plate-palette and then applies to the paper.

Color Spin

One of the art activities kids most request is color spin, in which the artist spins paint from a salad spinner or lazy Susan. Most artists are surprised how their design looks after the spinning stops. One try is never enough when spinning colors!

MATERIALS

salad spinner or lazy Susan (source from thrift shops and yard sales)
paper plates or other paper cut in circles
paints in squeeze bottles or in cups
spoons or droppers
marking pens
masking tape
scissors

Courtesy Catie Schneider, 2021

Art by child, age 4.
Courtesy Catie Schneider, 2021

PROCESS

Method One: Salad Spinner

1. Place a paper plate or other paper circle in the salad spinner.
2. Drop or squeeze paint dots or glops on the plate.
3. Crank up the salad spinner or spin by hand. The more you spin, the more the paint flies, making unusual designs and colors.
4. Stop the spinning and see what design has been made.
5. Adding more paint and going again with the same paper circle is perfectly fine!

Method Two: Lazy Susan

1. Place a paper plate or other paper circle on the lazy Susan. A loop of masking tape on the back of the paper will hold it in place.
2. Instead of paint, hold a marker in the drawing hand with the point touching the paper plate.
3. With the free hand, spin the lazy Susan manually while keeping the marker point touching. A design will form immediately. Change colors any time! Watch the colors move and blend. Spin backward and forward. Spin fast or slow.
4. When the spinning stops, check out the design. Want to add more? Keep on.

Art by Reid, age 5.
Courtesy Catie Schneider, 2021

EXTENSIONS

- Experiment with fast and slow speeds.
- Experiment with different types of pens, paints, and coloring tools.

Oil Pastel & Cotton Swabs

Oil pastels are bright and colorful drawing tools, offering many wonderful art experiences. In this version, the lines of an oil pastel drawing are touched by a cotton swab dipped in vegetable oil, breaking down the oil pastel lines and creating the effect of painting, but without paint.

Art by child, age 3.
Courtesy Jennifer Goodman Crowell, the Child Development Cooperative, Baton Rouge, LA

MATERIALS

oil pastels
strong drawing paper
vegetable oil

shallow cup or jar lid
supply of cotton swabs

PROCESS

1. Protect the work surface with newspaper or other covering because the vegetable oil tends to soak through the paper.
2. Draw on good drawing paper with oil pastels. (Good drawing paper works better than thin paper, such as newsprint or copying paper, because oil tends to soak through thinner paper.)
3. Draw anything: dots, shapes, scenes, pictures, or abstract designs. Anything the artist creates is just right for step 4.
4. When ready, dip a cotton swab in a shallow dish of vegetable oil, letting it soak up oil. Then rub the cotton tip on the oil pastel lines in the drawing, causing them to soften and become like paint. Push the colors around. Blend the colors, smooshing and smearing them. Use as many cotton swabs as needed.
5. Select a clean cotton swab and repeat blending and "painting" the oil pastel drawing. Note: Some lines may be left untouched, or if preferred, completely "paint" the entire drawing. There is no right way or wrong way to work with oil and oil pastels.
6. Let the drawing dry on newspaper or other drying area.

EXTENSIONS

- Explore using other base materials like:
  - back of an old poster
  - construction paper
  - heavy paper plates
  - square of plywood
  - textured paper
  - watercolor paper
- Draw on construction paper with a cotton swab dipped in oil. No oil pastels are needed. The paper will become translucent.

Baggie Painting

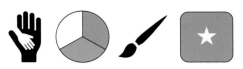

Several colors of tempera paint inside a resealable baggie become a nonmessy painting experience for young artists. Tape the baggie to a sunny window and explore the baggie with hands, smooshing and moving the paint about. The bright light will contribute to the colorful art experience.

MATERIALS

resealable baggie, quart or gallon
tempera paints, 2 or more colors
spoon
tape

PROCESS

1. Squirt or spoon several colors of tempera paint inside the baggie.
2. Seal well.
3. Tape the baggie at child height in a window with good light.
4. The young artist explores the baggie and paint with hands, moving the paint about, feeling the thickness of paint through the plastic, and pushing designs and patterns much like finger painting.

EXTENSIONS

- Try painting in a sandwich baggie, but seal well! The plastic is thinner than larger baggies.
- Make homemade finger paint (page 62) and use for baggie painting. Explore.
- Add food coloring to shaving cream, adding dollops to the ziplock baggie. Experiment.
- Add soft items to the paint in the baggie like pompoms or cotton balls. Try different items.
- Paint with a buddy, each with a baggie taped side by side in the window.
- Explore using soft-edged tools, such as the handle of a paintbrush or the bowl of a spoon. (Anything with points or sharp edges could tear the baggie.)

Art by Kali and Ben, age 4.
Courtesy Cindi Frakes Zieger, Sunny Days Preschool, 2021

Art by Ezra, age 3.
Courtesy Emma Koehler

Art by Claire, age 4, and Emery, age 2.
Courtesy Melea Martin, A Sense of Wonder Preschool and Daycare, Warren, OH, 2021

★★ 🖌 ◔ ✋ Ice Painting

Three different methods of painting with ice give artists three times the exploration, experimentation, and discovery! Method 1 involves painting on a block of ice, method 2 is painting on a plastic tub full of ice cubes, and method 3 explores painting with paint-cubes frozen on sticks. All methods require a freezer. Explore them all!

Courtesy Andrea Diuguid, 2021

METHOD ONE: BLOCK ICE

any freezer-safe pan or bowl — tray
water — tempera paints in cups
paintbrushes

Art by children, ages 2 and 3.
Courtesy Andrea Diuguid, 2021

1. Freeze a bowl or pan of ice. Plunk it out on a tray.
2. Artists paint the block of ice with brushes and tempera paints. Observe how paints thin and blend as the ice melts.

METHOD TWO: ICE CUBES IN A BIN

ice cubes made in trays or an ice maker — paintbrushes
plastic tub — tempera paints in cups

1. Fill a plastic tub to the top with ice cubes.
2. Artists paint on the cubes with brushes and tempera paints. Observe how the paints thin as the cubes melt, how the cubes jostle around, and how the paints blend.

METHOD THREE: PAINT WITH ICE CUBES

liquid watercolors — craft sticks cut in half or wooden ice-cream spoons
ice cube tray with individual sections — butcher paper or other choice of paper

Courtesy Andrea Diuguid, 2021

1. Pour a different color of liquid watercolor in each ice cube section. Fill all the sections, even if repeating colors.
2. Place a short craft stick or wooden ice-cream spoon in each section. Freeze.
3. Artists hold the cubes by their wooden handles and paint on paper.

4
Printing

Sponge Prints

Art by Nolan, age 6.
Brittany Dusek, 2021

Making prints with sponges is a basic art experience with many possibilities. Sponges can be cut in squares or cut with scissors into more complicated shapes. Dab the sponge into tempera paint of any color and then dab on paper. The design is up to the artist. A clothespin pinched on each sponge offers a less-mess painting handle.

MATERIALS

sponges cut in squares or other shapes
scissors
pinch-style clothespins, optional
tempera paints
pad of wet paper towels on a plate or tray
newsprint
paper

Art by Ben, age 4.
Courtesy Cindi Frakes Zieger, Sunny Days Preschool, 2021

PROCESS

1. Cut sponges into squares or other shapes.
2. Moisten sponges with water and then squeeze out water. The sponge should be moist but not dripping.
3. Pinch each sponge shape with a clothespin, which works as a painting handle. Otherwise, pinch the sponge between pointer and thumb.
4. Spread tempera paint on a pad of moist paper towels on a plate or tray. Several colors on the pad of paper will allow for mixing and blending. One color is also fine.
5. Dab the sponge into the paint on the paint pad. Then dab the sponge on the paper, making a sponge print. Several prints can be made before redabbing the sponge. Some artists will prefer to push and drag the sponge like they are painting with a brush. Others will make dabs and prints.

EXTENSIONS

*   Sponge print on other materials: fabric, wood, rocks, place mats, bookmarks.
*   Use sponge prints to create texture for the grass, fields, sky, or sea on a large mural.

Balloon Prints

What a great use for balloons saved from a birthday or celebration! Press a balloon in paint and then press it on paper. Surprising and delightful designs appear. Balloons filled tight with air make one kind of print, and balloons slightly out of air create a completely different kind of print. Explore the possibilities.

MATERIALS

balloons filled full or partially with air
tray or box lid with sides to hold balloons
tempera paint on a flat tray or plate (one or several colors)
paper

PROCESS

1. Collect balloons and place them on a tray or box lid with sides to keep them from rolling away.
2. Pour a puddle of tempera paint on a different tray or plate.
3. Press a balloon into the paint. Then press it on paper.
4. Press the balloon in trays with other colors of paint. Some artists like to mix colors of paint directly on the tray. Others will mix paint designs and colors on the paper.
5. Observe the print and the many tiny designs within each print.
6. Dry balloon prints overnight.

EXTENSIONS

- Make multiple prints with a balloon in each hand at the same time.
- Explore different printing motions: rolling, dabbing, sliding, bouncing, dropping.

Art by the toddler group, age 2.
Courtesy Melea Martin, A Sense of Wonder Preschool and Daycare, Warren, OH, 2021

Courtesy Bonita Sears, 2021

Upcycle Printing

Collect all kinds of "junk" and recyclables for making prints. Search the house, kitchen, classroom, garage, and recycle bin. Look for interesting shapes or textures when printed on paper. Mix some bright colors of tempera paint and make prints. When prints overlap other prints, new colors and new shapes appear. Artists are often completely surprised that an old worn toy or common kitchen utensil can make shapes such as hearts, bumpy circles, or perfect stop signs.

MATERIALS

A collection of recyclables, gadgets, or junk items to use for making prints:

buttons	feathers	leaves	scrap plastic	toothbrush
coins	foam shapes	lids	shells	toy pieces
cookie cutters	forks	pine cones	sponges	wire whisk
Duplos & Legos	hair curlers	pipe cleaners	spools	yarn
erasers	jars	plastic letters	sticks	
faux flowers	keys	rubber stamps	straws	

tempera paints or liquid watercolors in cups or a muffin tin
paintbrushes
paper
moist sponges or paper towels

Art by Otis, age 3.
Courtesy Kelly Hinds, 2021

PROCESS

1. Set the paints and brushes on the work space. Have paper towels or moist sponges nearby for wiping hands. Fill another tray or shallow box with the collected objects to be used for making prints.
2. Dip a paintbrush in paint and brush the object on the part a print will be made from. If preferred, a printing pad of paint color can be made by pouring a puddle of paint on a pad of moist paper towels.
3. Press the object on paper. Make many prints until the paint fades. Repaint the object to make more prints and designs and keep going.
4. Explore other items in the same manner. Watch for textures, shapes, and sizes. When all printing is complete, rinse and dry the objects. Consider keeping them stored for future printings.

Scrunch & Crumple Prints

The unique and varied patterns and designs discovered by scrunching and crumpling different materials offer surprise after surprise! Each scruncher ball makes a different kind of print when dipped in liquid watercolors and then pressed on paper.

MATERIALS

materials to scrunch and crumple into scruncher balls: newspaper, clear plastic wrap, aluminum foil, cotton fabric, plastic bag, paper bag
tray or box lid to hold all of the scruncher balls
liquid watercolors (or thinned tempera paints) in wide shallow bowls
paper for base: drawing paper, construction paper, butcher paper, paper plates

Courtesy Jennifer Goodman Crowell, 2021

Art by Evelyn, age 7, and Madelyn, age 4.
Courtesy Sunshine and Puddles Family Day Care, 2021

PROCESS

1. Scrunch and crumple different materials into balls. Scrunch them loose or scrunch them tight. Try any of the materials listed above, or find more materials and possibilities. Each scruncher ball will make its own unique pattern or design.
2. Set the balls in a tray or box lid on the work space.
3. Fill shallow bowls with liquid watercolors, each bowl a different color. It works well to assign each scruncher ball to one color, but artists are welcome to mix and blend in any way.
4. Dip a scruncher ball into one of the paint colors, and then press it on paper to make a print. Continue adding prints made by different scruncher balls in different colors. It's up to the artist whether to mix paint colors on a scruncher ball, directly on the paper or maintain one color for each ball.
5. The liquid watercolor prints should dry fairly quickly.

EXTENSION

Scrunch and crumple a square of white paper into a ball. Paint the outside edges of it with one color of liquid watercolors or tempera paint. Unfold it and then rescrunch the paper into a ball again. Paint the outside with a different color. Do this about three or four times. When the ball of paper is unfolded for the final time, it will have a unique tie-dye paint design that should cover most of the paper.

Courtesy Sunshine and Puddles Family Day Care, 2021

Finger Painting Monoprint

Finger painting is a basic art experience, but in this printing format, the usual exploratory "mess" is reduced significantly. Monoprinting is aesthetically and artistically interesting. Another benefit is that several artists can use the same printing setup with only a little additional moisture to extend the paint.

Art by Joy, age 4.
Courtesy Michelle Rasmussen, 2021

MATERIALS

liquid tempera paints

liquid starch

spoons

cookie sheet or smooth tray

paper

old towel

bucket of soapy water

newspaper

PROCESS

1. Pour a puddle of liquid starch in the center of the cookie sheet. Add a spoonful or two of liquid tempera paint. Add more than one color if you like. (No liquid starch? Use any homemade finger paint recipe or commercial finger paint product.)
2. The artist mixes the paint with hands directly on the cookie sheet and then spreads the paint to fill an area suitable for finger painting.
3. Finger paint on the cookie sheet, feeling and exploring the finger paint. Use fingers and hands to create designs, letters, words, pictures, or patterns.
4. When a design is ready, quickly rinse hands in the soapy bucket of water, and dry them with the old towel. Gently press a sheet of paper on top of the paint design, rubbing with very light pressure back and forth over the design.
5. Peel the paper from the finger painting design and see the design transferred to the paper. A second print, and sometimes even a third, can be made from the same finger painting. Place the painting on a sheet of newspaper to dry.
6. The next artist to use the cookie sheet will only need a little more liquid starch or some drops of water to freshen and moisten the paint. (Mixing colors on the cookie sheet can be intriguing.) More finger paint can be added at any time.

EXTENSION

Include tools in the painting experience to create even more patterns and design. Some suggestions are the edges of plastic gift cards, craft sticks, combs, pencil erasers, or rulers. Collect more tools that you think would be interesting to try.

1, 2, 3 Rubber Band Prints

Rubber bands stretched around cardboard squares create great prints. Using at least three colors of tempera paint expands the art and encourages new patterns and designs.

Courtesy Emma Koehler, 2021

Art by Ezra age, 3½.
Courtesy Emma Koehler, 2021

MATERIALS

3 cardboard squares, about 5 by 5 inches

handful of strong rubber bands

tempera paints, at least 3 colors

paintbrushes (regular or sponge)

paper

PROCESS

1. Cut cardboard to a workable size for the rubber bands to stretch tight but not break. Five to six inches square is usually about right. For this activity, three squares will be needed.
2. Wrap one rubber band around the cardboard. Is it tight? When satisfied, add several more rubber bands. They can cross over each other or lie in straight lines; they can be close together or farther apart. Experimenting with patterns will be part of the fun.
3. Make three boards with rubber bands in various patterns.
4. With a brush dipped in paint, paint the rubber bands on one board using one color only. The rubber bands should be well covered in paint. To make a print, press the painted bands down on a sheet of paper. Rub, rock, and press firmly. Then peel off the square to see the print.
5. Paint the second square with a different color. Press it down on the same sheet of paper so that colors and designs overlap. Peel off the board and see the results.
6. Ready to try a third color? Repeat the steps.
7. Dry the paper with its three overlapping prints, and continue making more prints. Experiment with the arrangement of the rubber bands and the paint colors. There will be many possibilities!

EXTENSION

Place a piece of paper in a small baking pan. Stretch rubber bands across the pan in any pattern. Paint the rubber bands with as many colors as you wish. Then snap or plunk each band to fling paint onto the paper inside the pan. Remove the paper through whatever space between bands works best. Then slide another piece of paper into the pan and continue.

Courtesy Emma Koehler, 2021

Wood Block Prints

Art by Brooks, age 5.
Courtesy Christine Kellerman, Anderson Prep Preschool, 2021

Art by Madeline, age 4.
Courtesy Christine Kellerman, Anderson Prep Preschool, 2021

Courtesy Christine Kellerman, Anderson Prep Preschool, 2021

There are natural patterns and designs ingrained in any block of wood—a wood block print will reveal these clearly! A scrap piece of lumber works well for this experience. Experiment with and compare the prints made with the smooth sides of the block and the rough ends of the block.

MATERIALS

damp paper towels
flat metal baking pan or tray
tempera paints
paintbrushes

block of wood with raised grain
    (a block sawed from a two-by-four
    piece of lumber works well)
paper

PROCESS

1. Place a pad of damp paper towels in metal baking pan or tray. Pour some tempera paint on the pad and spread it with a paintbrush. This will be the stamp pad. Add more than one color if you wish, or make several different stamp pads.
2. Press the rough, raised side of the block of wood on the pad of paint. Paint can also be brushed directly onto the wood with a paintbrush. Then press the block of painted wood onto a piece of paper. Press firmly.
3. Experiment with twisting and sliding the block as well as making a solid pressed print. Rocking the block is also a technique to try.
4. Try making prints with the smooth side of the wood block.
5. Continue making prints on new sheets of paper, exploring color and pattern possibilities.

EXTENSIONS

- Explore wood blocks or wood scraps of varying shapes, sizes, and grains.
- Glue shapes to a block with a variety of raised materials:
    – cardboard   – thick yarn   – craft foam   – stick-on furniture pads
- Wrap rubber bands, yarn, or string around and around a wood block.
- Print on white wrapping tissue or butcher paper to make wrapping paper.

Relief Stamp

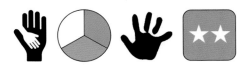

This easy relief-printing method makes a solid, precise print. Glue a cardboard shape or craft foam shapes on a square of cardboard. Paint the shape with tempera paints, and then press it down on paper. Rolling over the square with a brayer or rolling pin will clearly transfer the print. Explore overlapping and mixing different colors of paint on the paper.

MATERIALS

cardboard square
scissors
cardboard scraps or craft foam
   shapes

glue
tempera paint
moist paper towels in a tray or
   pan

paintbrushes
rolling pin or brayer
paper

PROCESS

1. Cut cardboard into a square about 6 by 6 inches. Other sizes of choice are fine as long as they are not too hard to manage—conside the size of your artists' hands. Adult help may be needed because cardboard is hard to cut.
2. Next cut a cardboard scrap into a shape. Glue the cardboard shape to the square of cardboard. The artist has a choice to use craft foam shapes alone or in addition to the cardboard shape. This square will be the stamp. Let the glue dry well before beginning the printing step.
3. Pour a puddle of tempera paint on a pad of moist paper towels in a flat pan or tray. Spread the paint out with a paintbrush. One color is enough, although multiple colors can be poured on the same pad. Several additional pads could be made, each with a different color.
4. Press the cardboard stamp into the paint pad.
5. Press the painted stamp down on a piece of paper. A great technique for strong prints is to roll over the back of the cardboard stamp with a rolling pin or brayer to ensure a more complete print.
6. Peel away the stamp to see the relief print. Make as many prints as desired.

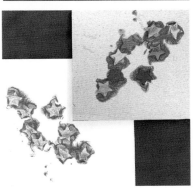

Courtesy MaryAnn Kohl 2021

EXTENSIONS

- Glue cardboard or foam shapes to a block of wood for an easy-to-hold printing tool.
- Create print designs following a theme or holiday:
  - pets   - seasons   - sports   - flowers   - birds   - holidays

String Block Art

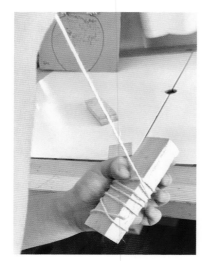

Try two methods for making prints with string and wood blocks. Method 1 suggests wrapping string around a block of wood to make a simple print with an easy design construction created in just minutes. Method 2 has the artist glue yarn or string in a design on a block of wood to make prints with more intention. Creativity blossoms when a single wood block can be turned into a variety of printing approaches.

MATERIALS

string or yarn
blocks of wood
glue in a dish

tempera paint (or liquid watercolors) in shallow pan
paintbrushes
paper

PROCESS

Method One: Wrapped-String Block

1. Wrap string around a block of wood enough times to create a pattern of string.
2. Pour paint in a shallow pan. Press the block into the paint so the string soaks up paint. (Or paint the string with a paintbrush.)
3. Make a print by pressing the string-block on paper. Press more than once to make several prints. Then repaint and print again.

Method Two: Glued-String Block

1. Soak string or yarn in glue in a dish. Arrange gluey strands on a block of wood. Long and short pieces can work together to create a design or picture. Dry overnight so the string or yarn is not wet and is very dry.
2. To make prints, press the string design into paint in a pan and then on paper. Make several prints. When the design fades, repaint and print again.

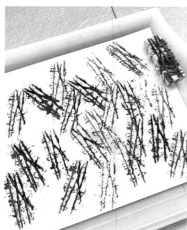

Courtesy Yvonne Tan, 2021

EXTENSIONS

- Wrap string around a cardboard tube, roll it through paint in a tray, and roll prints on paper. Rolling prints make continuous repeating designs. You can also glue string in a pattern on a cardboard tube, brush paint on the string, and roll prints on paper.
- Experiment with other materials that can be wrapped around a block of wood or glued to its surface for printing, such as ribbons, craft foam pieces, cardboard shapes, or fabric scraps.

Mini Mono-Prints

There are so many surprising print-making objects and utensils in the kitchen! Have fun searching for them and making prints. A muffin tin is particularly useful for process art: it's perfect for melting crayons, acting as a paint palette, or sorting loose parts and collage items. Now let's look at making mini-prints from the bottom of a muffin tin! Have squares of paper ready to catch the prints. If you save a muffin tin for art only, not for baking, there are no worries about returning it to a sparkling condition.

MATERIALS

muffin tin (any size)
tempera paints

paintbrushes
squares of paper, 4 by 4 inches

PROCESS

1. Turn the muffin tin over so the flat circles of the tin are facing up.
2. To begin, squirt or brush paint on one of the circles of the tin.
3. Then pat a square of paper on the paint.
4. Lift the paper and you will see a mono-print (*mono* means "one"). You can try to lift a second print from the same paint, but usually one is the most clear and bright.
5. Now paint other flat muffin tin circles. Squirt

or brush paint on the circles in any fashion. It's interesting to use a few different colors on each circle. The colors will mix when the paper is pressed on.
6. As before, pat a square of paper on each circle, lifting mono-prints from each.
7. Keep on with mixing colors and making prints. If you want to wash the muffin tin and start over, that's perfectly fine!
8. The prints will need to dry for a few hours.

EXTENSIONS

- Make prints from the right side up of the muffin tin, brushing paint all around the muffin cups but not in them. Lift prints from the areas with paint.
- Make a mono-print from the back of a textured cake pan, following the same steps as above.
- Mono-prints can be made on plastic trays, mirrors, table tops, bumpy sidewalks, and so on. Take some time to search out materials you'd like to try.

Courtesy May Hunter Scarmazzi, 2021

Glue Prints

Art by Henry, age 8.
Courtesy Megan Collins, 2021

Art by Henry, age 8, and Jamie, age 6.
Courtesy Megan Collins, 2021

Drawing with glue to make a design and then transferring that design to paper is like operating a simple printing press. The design works best if the glue lines are thickly squeezed from the glue bottle and then dried until completely hard.

MATERIALS

white glue in a squeeze bottle
heavy cardboard
paintbrush
thick tempera paint (or liquid
    watercolors) in a cup

white paper
spoon
newspaper

PROCESS

1. Draw with white glue from a squeeze bottle directly on the cardboard. Create a design or picture. Squeeze lots of glue to make thick lines.
2. Dry the glue design overnight or until completely dry, hard, and clear. Some designs take two nights.
3. With the paintbrush, paint thick tempera paint over the dry glue design.
4. Place a sheet of paper gently over the design. Rub the back of the paper with a spoon to make the design transfer to the paper. Use moderate pressure with the spoon. Peek under the paper to see how the transfer is going.
5. When ready, remove the paper, peeling from the corner. Place the print on a sheet of newspaper to dry completely.
6. Continue to make as many prints as you like.

EXTENSIONS

- Instead of a spoon, use gentle pressure of the hand to pat and rub the design through the paper.
- Experiment with different types of paper you have on hand: paper towels, tissue paper, coffee filter, cardstock, copying paper, cereal box, old poster

Spots & Dots

Printing dots and spots with a variety of tools has endless possibilities for designs, patterns, and even pictures! Collect items that might make dots or circle prints, such as the eraser on a pencil or the lid of a jar. Bingo bottles filled with paint make great dots and spots too. Spots and dots call for experimenting with round objects large and small.

MATERIALS

Items that make round print shapes:

balloon	cotton ball	elbow	golf ball	marker caps
bottle cap	dowel	eraser of a pencil	golf tees	nerf ball
bottom of a cup	drinking straw	fingertip	jar lids	pom-pom

tempera paints or liquid watercolors in shallow dishes or jar lids
paper

PROCESS

1. Pour tempera paint or liquid watercolors into several shallow containers or jar lids and place on the work space.
2. Arrange all the printing items on a tray within reach as well as a sheet of paper.
3. Dip a dot-printing item into paint, and then press on the paper. Make as many dots as possible from one dip in the paint. Change colors or change materials, but keep on going making dots and more dots! Fill the paper with dots in patterns and designs.

EXTENSIONS

- Learn about the great master, Georges Seurat, who is famous for a style of painting with dots called *pointillism*. Seurat combines dots of color with no lines, so when his art is viewed from a distance, the image appears to be solid. Visit the Art Institute of Chicago online and view Seurat's *A Sunday on La Grande Jatte*.
- The Sunday funnies and comic books have pictures that are created with dots of color. Use a magnifying glass and take a closer look.

Art by Clio, age 6.
Courtesy MaryAnn Kohl, 2021

Monograph

Monographing is a printing technique that starts with spreading paint on a tray and very lightly and gently covering the paint with a sheet of paper. The artist draws on the paper with a paintbrush handle to make marks, designs, or a picture. When the paper is peeled from the paint, the art will have transferred to the paper. The drawn design pushes a heavier layer of paint onto the paper giving artists a unique look at printing and design.

MATERIALS

tempera paint
liquid starch, optional
smooth surface for the paint: cookie sheet, table, plexiglass, plastic tray, baking pan

paintbrush
paper
paintbrushes with different size wooden handles

PROCESS

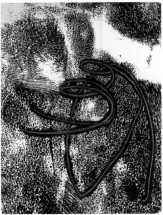

1. Mix tempera paint and liquid starch. Liquid starch helps smooth the paint. If you don't have any, just add a few drops of water to the cookie sheet with the tempera paint.
2. Cover a smooth surface such as a cookie sheet with a mixture of tempera paint and liquid starch. Several colors may be spread on the cookie sheet at one time. Use a paintbrush to smooth out the paint evenly.
3. Very lightly and gently lay a piece of paper on the painted cookie sheet. Do not press the paper into the paint. This step needs a very light touch.
4. With the end of a paintbrush handle, use heavy pressure and draw on the paper. Make lines, patterns, designs, or pictures.
5. Carefully peel the paper off the paint on the cookie sheet. Start at a corner and lift slowly.
6. The monograph design will be transferred to the paper. Results vary with this process of printing, so remember to work toward experimenting and exploring the process rather than look for "perfect" results.
7. Make additional prints from the same paint on the cookie sheet. Dry paint can be moistened with a spoonful of liquid starch, or add more paint and a few drops of water.

Art by child, age 4.
Courtesy Amy Kay, 2021

EXTENSION

Draw a design in the paint on the cookie sheet with a choice of tools. Some ideas are: fingers, paintbrush, cotton ball, cotton swab, pencil eraser.

Tree Rubbing Resist

Create a rubbing of tree bark with a melted disk of crayon called a scribble cookie (page 34). Other peeled crayons of all sizes are good to have handy. This rubbing incorporates a wax resist technique, giving the usual crayon rubbing a little twist. Once a tree rubbing has been captured with crayon on paper, head to the art table and wash over the rubbing with liquid watercolors or thinned tempera paints. The transformation of color will be a discovery showing how the wax in a crayon resists the water in paint.

MATERIALS

bag or box to carry supplies
outdoor area with trees
sheets of paper
scribble cookies or peeled crayons

liquid watercolors or thinned tempera paints in shallow cups, several colors
wide, soft paintbrush
foam paintbrush, optional

PROCESS

1. Collect scribble cookies, old crayons, and paper in a box, bag, or tote. Head outdoors and find a tree with textured bark. Set supplies down by the tree, and prepare to make the crayon rubbing.
2. Hold a sheet of paper on the bark of the tree with one hand, and rub a scribble cookie or other crayon over the paper with the other hand. The texture of the bark will appear as the crayon rubs across the paper. Try to get a bright rubbing. Don't be surprised if the paper has little holes in it from the job of rubbing crayon across the bumpy bark.
3. Walk about. Find more trees, and continue making rubbings of different tree barks.
4. When ready, gather all the art supplies and rubbings. Head back to the art area. Have liquid watercolors in shallow cups or tempera paints thinned with water ready to go. Be sure there is a wide soft paintbrush or a sponge brush ready too.
5. Dip the soft brush into a paint color, and then wash it across the crayon rubbing with wide strokes. Change colors or mix colors for each rubbing, or stick with one paint color. Notice how the crayon wax resists the water in the paint.
6. Dry all the tree rubbings. Compare the textures and colors when the paintings are dry.

Art by Leonard Kloiber, age 6.
Courtesy Janine Kloiber, 2021

Leaf Prints

The natural beauty and variety of leaves can be captured on paper by first painting on the leaf and then pressing a soft sheet of paper onto the painted leaf. When the paper is removed, a leaf print will remain. Make many prints from one leaf, exploring many colors.

Art by Montessori student, age 6.
Courtesy Jeanne Elser Smith, 2021

MATERIALS

strong, fresh leaf
newspaper
paintbrush
bar of hand soap
jar of water

liquid watercolor paints in shallow cups, or a watercolor paintbox
soft paper: white tissue paper, paper towels, copying paper, construction paper

PROCESS

1. Place the fresh leaf on a sheet of newspaper.
2. Dip a paintbrush in water, and then rub it on a wet bar of soap. This will help the watercolor paint stick to the leaf.
3. Dip the brush in paint. Paint a thick layer of paint on the leaf. Blend paint colors directly on the leaf.
4. Cover the painted leaf with a piece of soft paper. Rub and pat fingers gently on the paper to transfer the paint to the paper. Carefully peel away and remove the paper to see the leaf print.
5. Continue making leaf prints, exploring color combinations and types of paper.

Art by Amalia, age 4.
Courtesy Janine Kloiber, 2021

EXTENSIONS

- Paint with tempera paints instead of watercolors.
- Finger paint on a leaf.
- Press a piece of fabric on the leaf for a print. Try using fabric paints for fabric leaf prints.
- Make a leaf stencil by placing a leaf on paper and then dabbing paint on the leaf, spreading onto the paper. Remove the leaf and a stencil design will appear.

Playdough Impressions

Gather your favorite playdough, items to make impressions in the dough, and some paint and paper. Paint over the dough impressions with liquid watercolors or tempera paint. Pat a sheet of paper on the paint and rub gently. Peel the paper away, and there it is! A print has been transferred to the paper.

MATERIALS

playdough
rolling pin, optional
items to make impressions in the dough: cookie cutter, fingers, paintbrush handle, lace, wire grid, kitchen utensils, fork, paper clip, rim of a cup
liquid watercolors or tempera paint
sponge brush or other soft, wide brush
paper

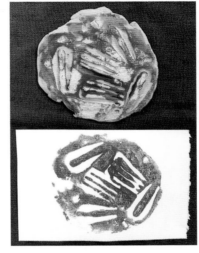

Courtesy MaryAnn Kohl, 2021

Art by child, age 4.
Courtesy Mary Turner, Mimi's House Family Childcare, 2021

PROCESS

1. Pat or roll out a ball of playdough so it is about ½ inch thick or more.
2. Press an item in the dough to make an impression. Press it well into the dough. Artists often like to fill the dough with many impressions, though some artists prefer only one. At this point, making playdough impressions may be enough. But if you want more, go to step 3.
3. Spread paint over the playdough and the newly made impressions.
4. Gently place a sheet of paper on the painted playdough. Pat and gently rub the back of the paper, but don't press too hard. Peel the paper from the dough and see the print that is transferred to the paper.
5. Add more paint in the same or a different color and make more prints.
6. When done, playdough can generally be rinsed quickly, patted dry, and used again. You can also blend in the paint colors by kneading them into the playdough.

EXTENSIONS

- Press a pattern in the dough using a wooden bead to make deep dots. Make a print.
- Press a fork with the tongs going up and down, and then press it going side to side next to the first impression. Continue alternating the up-down with the side-to-side, creating a pattern. Make a print.

Art by Zekiel, age 3.
Courtesy Mary Turner, Mimi's House Family Childcare, 2021

Bubble Prints

Printing with paint-colored bubbles is a happy art adventure. Like snowflakes, no two bubble prints are alike. With all that billowing bubbling color, be ready with a stack of paper to catch the prints.

MATERIALS

liquid dishwashing soap such as Dawn
wide-mouthed containers: cottage cheese, tall peanut butter jar, bowl, plastic picnic cups
tempera paints, liquid watercolors, or food coloring
tray with sides or box lid
paintbrush for stirring
beverage straws for each artist
stack of paper

PROCESS

1. Pour about ¼ cup dishwashing liquid into a wide-mouthed container. Make more than one container for different colors or several artists in a group.
2. Add paint or food coloring to the dishwashing liquid until the color is bright. Stir gently with a straw or paintbrush. Place the container on the tray with sides to help with spills.
3. Now to make the bubbles! Place one end of the straw in the container and the other end in the mouth. Blow in the straw. Do not suck in. The bubbles should billow and slightly flow over the edge of the container.
4. Apply a sheet of paper in a rolling motion over the bubbles for the bubbliest-looking prints. Try not to press down flat on the bubbles (although this still picks up a light print).
5. Repeat the bubble print process for bubbles of several colors on one paper.

EXTENSIONS

- Concentrated food coloring paste from the baking department makes bright bubble prints. Mix with a little water before adding it to the dishwashing soap.
- Cut out bubble prints and glue to other paper.
- Experiment with bubble prints on paper such as white wrapping tissue.

Art by Breanna, age 6.
Courtesy Cathy Bode, 2021

Art by Graham, age 6.
Courtesy Caitlin Rot, 2021

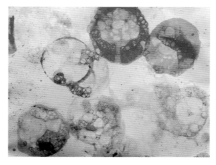

Art by Breanna, age 6.
Courtesy Cathy Bode, 2021

Footsie Prints

Look no further than little bare feet for this printing activity! A warm day would allow working outdoors where the mess is less, but a hallway or roomy kitchen will do. Be prepared for squeals and the sillies! Have an old towel and a tub of soapy water handy for easy cleanup of painted feet.

MATERIALS

long piece of wide butcher paper
rocks to hold down paper in the wind
tempera paints, mixed with liquid starch or a few
  drops of water
plastic containers to hold paint

big spoons, measuring cups with handles
old towels and a tub of soapy water
water source for cleanup
bare feet

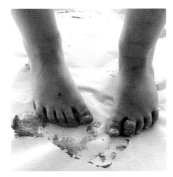

Art by Raegan, age 4.
Courtesy Amy Kay, 2021

PROCESS

1. Roll out the paper across the grass or playground. Place rocks on the corners to hold the paper in place.
2. Pour tempera paints in plastic containers. Put a spoon in each container. Small cups with handles, such as measuring cups, will be helpful for pouring paint too. Place them safely near the paper.
3. Set a tub of soapy water and old towels at the far end of the paper. A water source such as a hose will be helpful.
4. Spoon some puddles and blobs of tempera paint on the paper. Allow the artist to assist with color choices and placement.

5. Ready? Time for the artist to walk down the long roll of paper, stepping in paint and making prints. Mixing colors will happen naturally as well as intentionally. Paint can be slippery but is no cause for alarm. Be aware that some artists will feel like hopping, sliding, tiptoeing, dancing, and even crawling. Don't be surprised!
6. Add more paint and more prints. Add handprints too! Change the paper to a fresh roll if it gets too full of prints or has tears or holes from all the footwork.

Courtesy Janine Kloiber, 2021

EXTENSIONS

- Step in pans of paint and then walk on the paper.
- Make prints with rubber boots, shoes, and footwear with interesting patterns. Try to guess which artist, which shoe, or which foot made which print. Kids are very good at guessing.

Easy Sun Prints

To make a crisp, sharp image caused by the sun fading colored paper, it is very important that the objects on the paper do not move, and the day must be very sunny and bright with no wind or rain. Although this is the easiest and clearest sun print ever, be aware the faded sun-print paper will not last more than a day or two.

MATERIALS

materials collected from nature: leaves, ferns, rocks, pebbles, flowers, weeds, pine cones, twigs
bright papers: construction paper, colored poster board, colored butcher paper

flat tray
bright, dry sunny day
stones for weights
tape or glue

PROCESS

1. Go for a walk on a sunny day, collecting items from nature that have interesting shapes. Big leaves, graceful ferns, round pebbles, flower petals, and weeds are a few ideas.
2. Place a sheet of colorful construction paper on a flat tray in the shade. Try to be near the sunny area so carrying the art is quick and easy.
3. Arrange some of the nature items on the paper. Work quickly so the sun does not fade the paper! To keep the materials in place, if needed, use little pieces of tape or drops of glue but not enough to interfere with the design and print.

4. Carry the tray with paper and nature items out into the bright sun, somewhere safe and out of the wind. A picnic table is ideal! Set stones on the corners of the paper to hold if needed.
5. Leave the paper untouched until the sun sets. It's possible to leave it overnight unless there is too much dew or moisture. Bring the paper and nature items inside. Remove the items on the paper and observe the sun print with faded paper and unfaded shapes. The images will fade in a day or so, so save the paper for other art activities.

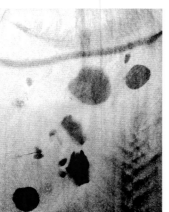

Art by Breanna, age 6.
Courtesy Cathy Bode, 2021.

EXTENSIONS

- Craft blueprint paper for kids can be purchased from school supply or hobby stores for making quality sun prints.
- Tape or pin objects to a bulletin board covered with bright butcher paper. Check in seven days, remove the objects, and observe the prints.
- Explore sun prints from everyday items such as scissors, a brick, a fork, or a hammer.

Rolling Pin Printing

A rolling pin wrapped with a textured material such as bubble wrap or thick yarn will roll a textured print across big paper. Explore other wrapping materials such as crumpled foil or shelf liner.

MATERIALS

rolling pin

textured materials: bubble wrap, thick yarn, long weeds, burlap, crumpled aluminum foil, heavy twine, long grass, net vegetable bag, rubber shelf liner, large, supple leaf, strip of thick fabric, lace

tape, optional

tempera paint or liquid watercolors in a flat pan with low sides

paintbrushes

large paper, such as craft paper or butcher paper

PROCESS

Wrap the rolling pin with a chosen material. Tape may be needed to secure the loose edges. As the project progresses, explore more than one wrapping material to see the possibilities. Hint: Cover the rolling pin in plastic wrap to protect it from paint stains.

Method One: Dip and Roll

1. Fill a flat pan with a shallow amount of paint. Choose one color or several colors.
2. Roll the wrapped rolling pin in the paint, coating all sides.
3. Roll the painted rolling pin across the large paper. If the paper is big enough, keep rolling and rolling to create a long, repeating pattern.
4. Then reroll in paint and keep rolling!

Method Two: Puddle Roll

1. Drop puddles of paint on the large paper in any pattern or design. Use as many colors as desired.
2. Roll the wrapped rolling pin directly through the paint puddles, spreading a repeating design across the paper. If the paper is large enough, keep rolling and rolling to create a long, repeating pattern.
3. Add more paint puddles to the paper and keep rolling!

Art by Adalynn Goodman, age 2.
Courtesy Heather Ann Goodman, 2021

EXTENSION

Explore rolling a paint design with the paper on the wall instead of the floor, grass, or table.

Oil Marbling

It's true, oil and water don't mix—but they make beautiful marbled paper in an easy, safe way for young artists' hands and minds. Although this method can be a bit messy, the marbled designs are swirly and patterned in perfect marbling style and worth the exploration.

MATERIALS

vegetable oil
liquid watercolors
small cups, one for each color
clear baking dish
water
squares of cardstock or watercolor paper
fine grade glitter, optional

more helpful utensils:
  forks
  spoons
  chopsticks
  craft sticks
  droppers
  pipettes

PROCESS

1. Pour a little vegetable oil in a small cup. Add one color of liquid watercolors to the oil. Whisk and stir with a fork. Then make several more cups of oil and paint, each a different color.
2. Fill a clear baking dish with water about 1 inch deep.
3. To begin the marbling steps, spoon a little of the oil and watercolor mixture on the water in the baking dish. A dropper or pipette is another method for adding oil and color to the water. Add one color to the water or add many. Gently swirl the colors or leave as is.
4. Gently lay a square of cardstock on the water. Lightly press on the paper until it is fully touching the water. Then immediately lift it from the water, letting water drip back into the baking pan.
5. Lay the marbled paper on newspaper to rest and begin drying.
6. Now add more colors to the same water, and make another marbled print. Keep going until the water becomes too murky. Then get fresh water and keep marbling! Add glitter if the artist wishes!
7. Each square of marbled cardstock should dry flat because it can be drippy. When it's dry, it won't be as oily and can be used for other art ideas.

Art by Graham, age 6.
Courtesy Caitlin Rot, 2021

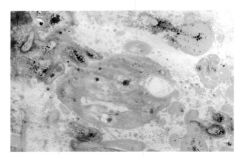

Art by Madison, age 5.
Courtesy Christine Kellerman,
Anderson Prep Preschool, 2021

5
Sculpture & Modeling

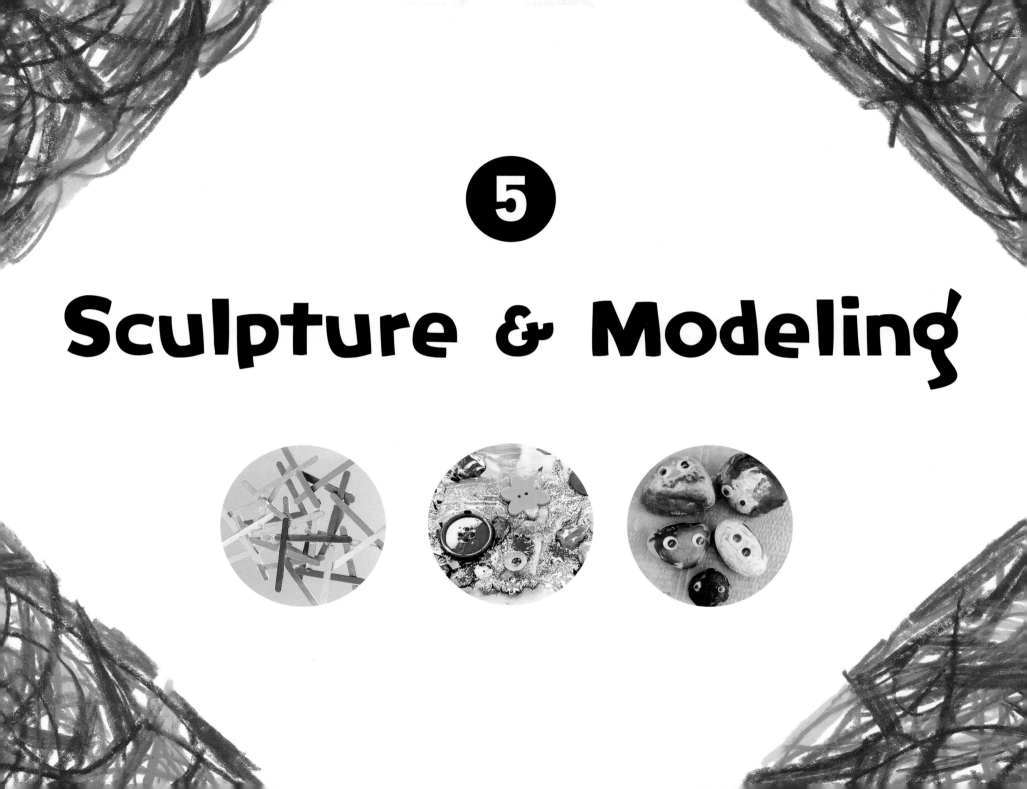

Hanging Box Sculpture

Collect small boxes of all kinds. Wrap them with white butcher paper or plain wrapping paper. Young artists then paint the boxes with liquid watercolors. Decorate the boxes with gems, sequins, glitter glue, and other collage materials. Hang the boxes with twine from the ceiling, a tree, or any overhead choice.

MATERIALS

boxes of all sizes
paper: butcher paper, craft paper, plain giftwrap
    paper, white wrapping tissue
twine
glue, tape
liquid watercolors, several colors in shallow
    containers

paintbrushes
scissors
shiny and interesting decorating materials: gems,
    buttons, foil stickers, sequins, broken jewelry,
    glitter glue, spangles, glitter, aluminum foil
    pieces, paper clips

PROCESS

1. Cover boxes with paper like you are wrapping a gift. (It's also OK to skip the wrapping step and paint/decorate the boxes as is.) Tape the paper to hold. Cut any excess paper with scissors.
2. This is a good time to slip some twine into the paper and tape well for hanging the boxes later. Note: Some artists can do the wrapping on their own. Others will need help.
3. Artists paint the boxes with liquid watercolors, which will dry fairly quickly. Paint all sides or choose to paint on one side only.
4. Decorate the boxes with shiny collage materials, glitter glue, buttons, and so on. To decorate all sides, plan to let one side dry before flipping it over to do another side. The artist can do five sides, and the sixth side will have to wait for some drying time. It is also perfectly fine to only decorate one side.
5. When dry, hang the boxes from the twine from a ceiling, eaves, a tree, or other overhead area.

EXTENSIONS

- Decorate the boxes with a theme design, such as sports or holidays. Pictures can be cut out to glue on the boxes to further the theme decoration.
- Draw with markers directly on the boxes instead of paint, or in addition to paint.

Art by child, age 4.
Courtesy Zannifer Rolich, 2021

Wood Scrap Sculpture

Wood scraps are treasures with their beauty, originality, textures, and aromas. Scraps from a custom picture frame shop are incredibly varied and unique. Some of the pieces have gold paint, others have fabric embedded in the frame, and still others have carvings that make them little works of art. Artists can use the strangely shaped pieces that come from a woodshop class, especially if there are jigsaw pieces in curves and squiggles. Glue them together on a base, and the sculpture is complete.

MATERIALS

wood scraps:
    framing scraps from a picture frame shop
    construction site wood scraps
    lumber yard pieces
    woodshop class scraps
base about 12 inches square:
    plywood, cardboard, strong paper plate,
    pizza circle
white glue or craft glue

masking tape, optional
glue gun, with supervision, optional
coloring medium:
    tempera paint, liquid watercolors, crayons,
    markers
collage items:
    yarn, ribbons, magazine pictures, sewing
    scraps, feathers, glitter, confetti

PROCESS

1. Choose a sturdy base, such as a square of plywood or cardboard.
2. Place framing scraps and other scraps of wood on the work space within easy reach.
3. Begin building a sculpture on the base by stacking, arranging, and testing out the scraps.
4. When ready, begin gluing the scraps together with white glue or craft glue. If the glue won't hold, use masking tape to help until the glue dries. Remove the tape when glue holds. (An adult may assist with a glue gun, completely supervised.)
5. When satisfied with the sculpture and sculpture is completely dry, the pieces may be painted, colored, or decorated with collage items, crayons, pens, or paint. The sculpture may also be left as the original design.

Courtesy Megan Harney, 2021

Stick & Straw Build

Art by Shoshana, age 12.
Courtesy MaryAnn Kohl, 2021

Building with sticks and straws has infinite possibilities for the artist who likes a sculpture that grows quickly and stands on its own. Save drinking straws, coffee stir sticks, juice straws, and other craft sticks. Join then together with masking tape to build an imaginative sculpture.

MATERIALS

collect and recycle sticks and straws:

coffee stir sticks	tongue depressors
drinking straws (plastic, paper, bendy)	craft sticks
coffee straws	popsicle sticks
wooden ice-cream spoons	chopsticks

masking tape or other tape

other joining materials, optional: stickers, labels, pipe cleaners

PROCESS

1. Join sticks and straws together with masking tape. Sometimes it helps to tear off multiple pieces of tape and stick them to the edge of the table before beginning so that the sculpture can be created more quickly.
2. Straws and some sticks can be shaped, cut, and bent. To make a straw longer, pinch one end and slip it into another straw, no tape needed. Explore and experiment with the sticks and straws while constructing the sculpture.
3. When satisfied with the sculpture, the work is complete.

EXTENSIONS

- Tape or glue the sculpture to a base, such as a paper plate, block of wood, or cardboard.
- Add collage or decorative items to the sculpture, such as yarn, pasta, glitter, buttons, or paint.

Upcycle Sculpture

Part of the creativity of building a sculpture in a block of Styrofoam is saving and choosing the materials and imagining how they might be used. A simple pipe cleaner can be curled and bent. Two nails held together by a strand of braided yarn are inventive. In other words, creating with saved materials is highly imaginative. Saving, recycling, and collecting can take part over time as you wait for the right sculpture activity.

Art by Clara, age 5.
Courtesy Christine Kellerman, Anderson Prep Preschool, 2021

MATERIALS

foam blocks for the base:
   Styrofoam packing blocks, such as those appliances are shipped in
   foam cooler chest or lid
   foam insulation sheet, scored and snapped into blocks (from a hardware store)
collage items to add to the sculpture:

beads	corks	jewelry	plastic flowers
broom straws	cotton balls	macaroni, pasta	ribbons
burrs	craft sticks	magazine pictures	sewing scraps
cattail fluff	embroidery floss	photographs	tissue paper scraps
chopsticks	fabric scraps	pine cones	wire
coffee stir sticks	feathers	pipe cleaners	yarn

Art by Henry, age 5.
Courtesy Christine Kellerman, Anderson Prep Preschool,2021

PROCESS

1. Begin by sticking chosen saved materials into a block of Styrofoam or other foam block. Arrange, remove, rearrange, and create.

2. Add collage materials to the sculpture.
3. Build and build!

Art by Madison, age 5.
Courtesy Christine Kellerman, Anderson Prep Preschool,2021

EXTENSIONS

Build a theme sculpture:
– "Things I Collected on My Walk"   – hardware   – red only (color sculpture)
– seasons   – "Things I Like"   – holiday (Christmas, July 4th, Father's Day, and so on)

Loose Arrangement

Art by Claire, age 4.
Courtesy Melea Martin, A Sense of Wonder Preschool and Daycare, Warren, OH, 2021

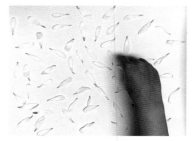

Art by Montessori student, age 3.
Courtesy Jeanne Elser Smith, 2021

Art by Vega, age 5½.
Courtesy Vidya Rao, www.amotherspensieve.wordpress.com, 2021

Over time, collect interesting items that can be used for a loose arrangement, such as shells, pebbles, bottle caps, and corks. The base of the arrangement can be paper, scrap wood, driftwood, a tray, or other material of choice. A loose arrangement is just that: it has its artistic moments when arranged, and then it is disassembled and items are reused at another time. No glue is needed!

MATERIALS

base:

cardboard	driftwood	paper
cardboard box	newspaper	tray
dirt or sand	old poster	scrap of wood

loose parts:

beads	confetti	flower petals	shells
bottle caps	corks	leaves	stickers
broken jewelry	dry beans	paper clips	toy parts
buttons	fabric scraps	pebbles	
can flip-tops	feathers	seeds	

PROCESS

1. Place the chosen base material on the work space, and then set up the loose materials in separate containers within easy reach.
2. Work on a base for the arrangement. Arrange the loose materials in any pattern or design. They are not glued in place, so the choices are endless and constant.
3. Move them about. Shake the base and disrupt them! Arrange again.
4. The same loose arrangement can be worked on for many days, adding and taking away, rearranging, and so on.
5. At some point, the loose items can go back into their containers to save for another activity or art exploration.

EXTENSIONS

- Glue the items in place for a permanent arrangement.
- Arrange a design with materials that are not saved, such as fresh flower petals and leaves.

Foil Sculpture

Crumpling a sheet of aluminum foil into a shape is a new way of modeling for most young artists, so very different from playdough or clay. For the strongest, longest-lasting sculpture, try to make the art out of one large piece of foil instead of joining several small pieces of foil. However, smaller pieces can be added if needed.

MATERIALS

aluminum foil
tape, optional
stapler, optional
cardboard covered with foil for base, optional

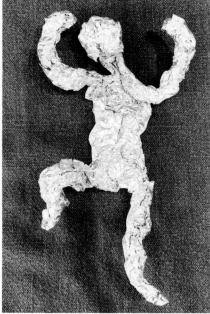

PROCESS

1. Crumple aluminum foil and shape it into any form or object. Tearing the sheet of foil seems to be a natural part of creating the sculpture.
2. The longest lasting sculptures are made with one large piece of foil. If additional pieces of foil must be used, join with tape or a stapler. (Older artists can use straight pins.)
3. Carefully bend the sculpture in different poses if desired.
4. The sculpture can be mounted on a base, or left freestanding.

EXTENSIONS

- Combine paper and crumpled foil to create a paper foil sculpture.
- Foil can be painted with tempera paint. Add a few drops of dishwashing detergent to the paint, which will help the paint adhere to the foil.
- Create foil puppets on sticks.
- Permanent markers can add a bit of color and design to foil, though markers tend to "give up" marking on foil after moderate use.

Courtesy MaryAnn Kohl, 2021

Box Sculpture

Courtesy Demaris Weitzel, 2021

Collecting an assortment of cardboard and boxes for a sculpture is almost as interesting as building the sculpture itself. Start assembling the boxes with tape, glue, or other materials. The sculpture will grow and expand quickly before the eyes. Painting or decorating is optional.

MATERIALS

cardboard and boxes:

beverage case box	egg cartons	pizza box
big ice-cream containers	jewelry box	recycled paper
box lids	milk cartons	shoebox
cardboard tubes	oatmeal box	takeout food containers
copying paper box	paper cups	

tape: masking tape, cellophane tape, duct tape
other materials for binding: stapler, rubber bands, labels, stickers
glue gun, with adult supervision, optional
paints and brushes, optional

PROCESS

1. Collect an assortment of boxes and containers made of cardboard or paper. Smaller pieces of cardboard, poster board, and recycled paper can also be collected.
2. Glue, tape, staple, and bind boxes together, letting the design of the artwork take shape as it grows.
3. When the sculpture is complete, paint and decorate if desired. Dry.

EXTENSIONS

- Add collage materials: string, yarn, feathers, ribbons, sewing scraps, pom-poms.
- Build a box sculpture with other concepts:
  - totem pole
  - cabin or fort
  - dinosaur
  - for toys to play on
  - very tall
  - with paper cups

T. rex art by Emmeline, age 3.
Courtesy Demaris Weitzel, 2021

Branch Sculpture

A branch sculpture is especially versatile and creative because the materials chosen to design the branch can be changed seasonally or can be created to go with a theme or special day. This sculpture can be an ongoing, permanent art addition with changing decorations and creations for any classroom or home.

MATERIALS

branch without leaves, 2 to 3 feet tall
large coffee can, bucket, or other similar container
sand
collage items and sculpture materials:

colored wire	photographs	small boxes
glitter	pine cones	string
holiday ornaments, child-made	pipe cleaners	tissue blossoms
paper scraps	ribbon	yarn

Art by Zekiel, age 3.
Courtesy Mary Turner, Mimi's House Family Childcare, 2021

PROCESS

1. Find a tree branch without leaves but with small offshoots, about 2 to 3 feet tall.
2. Set the branch deep into a large coffee can filled with sand. The sand will help keep the branch upright.
3. Make decorations of any kind to hang from the smaller branches.
4. Add to or change the decorations at any time.

EXTENSIONS

- Make seasonal decorations, such as spring flowers, autumn leaves, Independence Day flags, and paper snowflakes. Change the decorations when the holiday or season ends.
- Wrap and weave the branch with fabrics, ribbons, and yarns to make a weaving. Other materials can also be added to the weaving, such as dry grasses, paper strips, or leaves.
- Add permanent hanging loops of pipe cleaners or wire so changes of decorations or ornaments can take place quickly and easily. The loops can be left on the branch at all times.
- Instead of sand, stabilize the branch by pouring plaster of Paris into the coffee can. Stick the branch into the plaster before it dries and hold in place until the plaster sets.

Garlands

Artists can create imaginative garlands from almost anything lightweight that can be pierced and threaded with colorful yarn, which can then draped about the room for special occasions or everyday enjoyment. Smaller garlands also make festive necklaces.

MATERIALS

plastic darning needle, optional
thread, twine, yarn, embroidery floss, or string
masking tape, white glue, or nail polish
paper and lightweight materials:

art tissue, scraps or cut in shapes	crepe paper scraps	packing peanuts	ribbon
	cupcake liners	paper scraps	spools
buttons	drinking straws, cut into segments	pasta with holes & tubes	
collage items			

Art by Connor, age 7.
Courtesy Melea Martin, A Sense of Wonder Preschool and Daycare, Warren, OH, 2021

PROCESS

1. Prepare the needle and yarn: Wrap a piece of tape around the end of the yarn or string to make a simple needle. Or, dunk the end of the yarn or string in white glue or clear nail polish. Let it set until hard. A third choice is to thread a plastic darning needle, which has a large eye. Keep yarn or thread to a comfortable length, from 12 inches to 36 inches, depending on the age or skill of the artist.
2. Any object with a hole in it or light enough to have a hole made in it is suitable for threading a garland. Begin threading materials in a random fashion or with a planned pattern.
3. When one string is filled, tie a knot and then tie it to another string to make a longer garland.

Many individual garlands can be joined to make one very long, colorful display.

4. Hang from the ceiling in a draping fashion or around windows or doors.

Art by Abby, age 8.
Courtesy Melea Martin, A Sense of Wonder Preschool and Daycare, Warren, OH, 2021

EXTENSIONS

- Follow a self-made pattern of threading such as two yellow flowers, one bead, one straw, two yellow flowers, one bead, one straw, and so on.
- Create a flower necklace with art tissue flowers and cupcake liners, with straws to separate them. Use elastic cord.
- Create a holiday garland for Christmas, Valentine's Day, Halloween, or other events.

Stick & Watercolor Hanging 🖐 ◔ ⛫ ★★

Paint craft sticks with liquid watercolors, and join them together with glue, one to another, in any design or shape. Hang the entire stick design from a stick or dowel with twine or yarn.

MATERIALS

craft sticks, tongue depressors
liquid watercolors
paintbrushes of any size
jar for rinsing

white glue
string or twine
stick or dowel

PROCESS

1. Paint craft sticks with liquid watercolors. They will dry fairly quickly.
2. Join the sticks together with glue. It works well to arrange them on a flat surface so they can dry and hold well. Other options for gluing and drying are also possible, like using a cool glue gun with adult supervision.
3. When the painted sticks are holding together well, tie a string to them. Then tie the string to a stick or dowel so the design hangs from the stick.
4. Add additional string to the stick or dowel so it can support the hanging sculpture.

EXTENSIONS

- Decorate the craft sticks with glitter, sequins, stickers, bits of art tissue, and so on.
- Hang the sculpture with shiny ribbon or natural-looking raffia strands.
- Add additional hanging items of choice from the dowel, such as cardboard shapes, wooden spools, metal washers, pine cones, and buttons.

Art by Joe, age 8, and James, age 4.
Courtesy Sue Gaudnyski, Art in Miss G's Garden, 2021

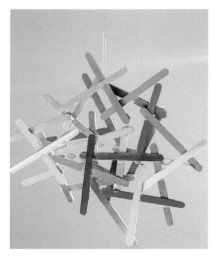

Courtesy Christie Burnett, Childhood 101, 2021

Edible Sculpture Board

Art by Zekiel, age 3, and friend, age 4.
Courtesy Mary Turner, Mimi's House Family Childcare, 2021

Courtesy Mary Turner, Mimi's House Family Childcare, 2021

Many foods lend themselves to artful arrangement. Designing with food makes it appeal more to hungry artists when it becomes part of a meal, snack, or party treat. Create a sculpture board that is creative and tasty, and especially suitable for a get-together or party.

MATERIALS

cardboard square or heavy paper plate
aluminum foil
tape
spreading knife
muffin tin or small cups
scissors, optional
ingredient for spreading, joining, and sticking:
    frosting, cream cheese, peanut butter,
    other seed or nut spreads

some suggestions of foods for creating the sculpture board:
    fruits: blueberries, strawberries, watermelon, raisins, grapes
    vegetables: carrots, celery, cherry tomatoes
    candy: M&M's, chocolate chips, butterscotch chips, Hershey's Kisses, gumdrops
    snacks: pretzels, crackers, animal crackers, mini marshmallows, trail mix

PROCESS

1. Cover the cardboard with aluminum foil, folding and pressing loose edges to the back. Tape the loose edges on the back to hold.
2. Begin by spreading some of the joining and sticking ingredient on the foil board. Press a food item into it, adding more if needed to hold the food in place.
3. Continue adding foods in any way. Some artists will make a pattern, others a face or picture, and still others will employ random placement.
4. Cover the board with foods until satisfied with the result. Then enjoy immediately as a treat.

EXTENSION

Create a lunch sculpture board with sandwich combinations, such as cheese and carrot circles, peanut butter and jelly designs, bread squares or shapes, and crackers.

Rock Tracing

The artist traces around a rock that is about the size of one's hand. Cover the paper with overlapping traced rock shapes. Then color in the shapes with markers, paint, or crayons.

MATERIALS

smooth rock, about the size of a child's hand
water in a tub
towels
paper of any kind
markers, pencils, pens, or crayons
coloring tools: markers, tempera paint, liquid watercolor, crayons, oil pastels
paintbrushes, if using paint

PROCESS

1. Find a smooth rock that is easy to hold. Wash the rock in the tub of water and dry with a towel.
2. Place the rock on the paper, hold it steady, and trace around the rock.
3. Move the rock and keep tracing. Overlap rock tracings. Fill the paper.
4. When ready, paint or color the traced shapes. Watch for overlapping shapes and decide how to color those areas too.
5. If using paint, dry the rock tracing art.

EXTENSIONS

- Color the rock tracing with bright, heavy crayon or oil pastels. Then wash over the art with thinned tempera paint or liquid watercolors, creating a wax resist.
- Cut out the rock tracing and hang from yarn from the ceiling. Consider coloring both sides of the tracing.
- Trace other found objects and repeat the general steps of rock tracing.

Art by Josephine, age 4.
Courtesy Janine Kloiber, 2021

Rock Buddies

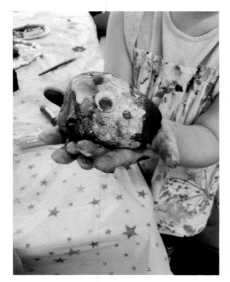

Collect rocks and stones. When washed and dried, paint and decorate the rocks as individual rock buddies, each with a personality and look of its own. Each rock shape also contributes to the personality of the buddy. Don't forget the googly eyes!

MATERIALS

rocks and stones

water in a tub

towels

tempera paints and brushes

jar of water for rinsing brushes

permanent markers, optional

googly eyes

glue

yarn

PROCESS

1. Collect rocks and stones with interesting shapes. Wash them in water and dry them with a towel.
2. Choose one rock to begin, and paint it with tempera paint. Any colors or designs are welcome.
3. Continue to paint all the rocks in any pattern or colors. Let them all dry briefly before decorating them with markers or other materials.
4. Glue on some googly eyes. Draw more features with permanent markers.
5. Yarn can be added for hair or decoration.
6. Dry rock buddies overnight.

EXTENSIONS

- Part of the fun is naming the rock buddies. They are, after all, buddies!
- Glue pieces of felt to a rock buddy to change it into a rabbit, dog, cat, or imaginary creature.
- Collect driftwood or scraps of wood blocks and create wood buddies.

Courtesy Nancy Valentine, minimarkmakers.com, 2021

Rock Stacking

Simply stack rocks! That's it! Working outdoors is ideal, though rocks can be brought inside as well. Artists learn quickly that larger, flat rocks at the base of the stack, getting smaller as they go, make the tallest stacks. Stacking rocks outdoors should not be a permanent project. Be considerate of the environment and return rocks to their original location when done.

MATERIALS

flat rocks and stones of all kinds
outdoor area

PROCESS

1. Collect rocks in one area outdoors.
2. Stack rocks, making a tower of at least three rocks if possible. Can it be taller? Higher?
3. When the stacking is complete and the artwork appreciated, return the rocks to their original locations.

EXTENSIONS

- Add pebbles, shells, or bits of wood to the stacking.
- Save smaller stones in a basket. Make a stacking of rocks indoors. Enjoy the stones as loose materials or glue them together to make a more permanent stack.
- Paint the rocks or stones if creating an indoor sculpture. Add glitter or other art materials as desired.

Art by child, age 5.
Courtesy Karen Begley, www.natureplaystudios.com, 2021

Art by Rylin, age 9.
Courtesy Ronda Harbaugh 2021

Classic Goop

Art by children, age 2.
Courtesy Jennifer Goodman Crowell, the Child Development Cooperative, Baton Rouge, LA

Goop is not a traditional art experience, but it is so strange, compelling, amazing, and thought provoking that it cannot be ignored. When colorings are added and explored in the Goop, the mixing, blending, and swirling of the colors adds to the sensory experience of exploring such an unusual mixture.

MATERIALS

The mixture of Goop is always 2 parts cornstarch to 1 part water. The following recipe is good for one or two artists to explore the material in a flat baking pan. Larger batches can be made for a water table, tub, or small plastic wading pool.

    ½ cup cornstarch and ¼ cup water (2:1 ratio)
    measuring cup
    food coloring or thin tempera paint in cups
    tray, bowl, spoon, or pan
    9-by-12-inch baking pan

PROCESS

1. Mix the recipe of cornstarch and water in a measuring cup.
2. Pour into a 9-by-12-inch baking pan.
3. Explore and observe the Goop with bare hands. There is no finished product, just the process of exploring a strange and delightful mixture.
4. Add a few drops of food coloring or thin tempera paint to the mixture and mix in with the hands. The mixing, blending, and swirling of colors is a fully vibrant part of exploring Goop.
5. When finished, the mixture can be stored in an airtight container and reused. Add a bit of water if it dries out.
6. Wash hands and clean up.

EXTENSIONS

- Make an extralarge batch of Goop in a tub for many hands to explore together.
- Experiment with other materials to color the Goop, such as crushed chalk, crayon shavings, Jell-O, or powdered drink mixes.

Playdough

Playdough is THE most basic and important modeling experience for children of all ages and experience levels. There are many playdough recipes—some difficult and some easy—but the following one is always successful. It has smooth consistency and extended life, holds indentations and shapes, and doesn't stick to hands like some recipes do. Store the playdough in an airtight container in the refrigerator when not in use, although keeping it on the shelf works fine too. Allow for exploration and experimentation.

MATERIALS

Mix and cook the following ingredients in a saucepan on low heat until a ball forms.
Use a wooden spoon to mix and stir:

1 cup flour	1 cup salt
1 cup water	1 tablespoon cream of tartar (optional, for freshness)

If adding color to the dough, stir into the water before mixing. Choose from:

crushed colored chalk	powdered beverage mix	tempera paint
food coloring	juice from boiled foods like beets,	Jell-O
liquid watercolor	cranberries, onion skins	

Assemble a choice of utensils to work with dough. Some suggestions are:

cookie cutters	garlic press	plastic knife	small hammer
dowel	jar lid	plastic letters	toy parts
fork	kitchen tools	rolling pin	

Art by Hilde, age 3.
Courtesy MaryAnn Kohl, 2021

PROCESS

1. Prepare the playdough recipe.
2. Begin exploring the dough while it is still warm, or place in the refrigerator to cool and explore later. Roll, pound, stretch, pinch, pat, cut, twist, and explore the characteristics and possibilities of playdough.
3. When finished, place the dough in a plastic container with a snap-on lid and store in the refrigerator for up to two weeks, or on the shelf for several days.

EXTENSIONS

- Whatever the artist imagines, discovers, explores, or experiments with is an important part of the joy and versatility of playdough.
- Some days use only hands with playdough. Other days add tools and utensils.
- Make play dough impression prints, page 87.

Soda Cornstarch Dough

Some unusual qualities make this dough recipe a good choice for modeling: it is pure white and hardens quickly, can be easily doubled, stores well in an airtight container for several weeks, models very well, and paints nicely too.

MATERIALS

1 cup baking soda
½ cup cornstarch
⅔ cup warm water
saucepan, stove, spoon

food coloring or tempera paint
board
paintbrushes, optional

PROCESS

1. Prepare the dough: Mix 1 cup baking soda and ½ cup cornstarch in a saucepan. Add ⅔ cup warm water and stir until smooth. Cook over medium heat, stirring until the consistency is like mashed potatoes.
2. Pour onto a board to cool. Then knead. Note: For color, knead coloring into the dough until blended, or paint finished dough sculptures later with tempera paint, markers, or other color supplies.
3. Explore, model, and play with the dough. However, take note that the dough dries quickly. The artists can make whatever they wish. Then let the dough air-dry until hard.
4. When objects are dry, the objects may be further colored or painted. For a shiny coat, wait until the objects are fully dry and then brush with thinned white glue. Let dry again.

EXTENSIONS

- Mix up several batches of different colored doughs and create holiday ornaments or decorations. For instance, twisting a red snake with a white snake will make a candy cane ornament. Or three white balls joined one on top of the other with other dough parts added could be a snowman.
- Make a set of storybook characters or puppets and stick them on bamboo skewers. When they are dry, make up a puppet show.

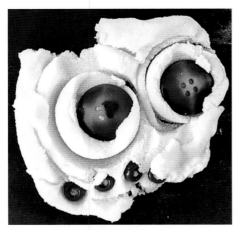

Art by child, age 4.
Courtesy Jennifer Goodman Crowell, the Child Development Cooperative, Baton Rouge, LA

Courtesy Demaris Weitzel, 2021

Salt Cornstarch Dough

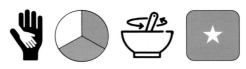

This amazing dough is an especially great cooked mixture because it uses so few ingredients and hardens relatively quickly. It can also be "speed dried" in the oven at 200°F for 1 hour. The texture is grainy, and the appearance is pure white. Work with the dough while it is still warm from the stove for an added tactile sensory experience.

MATERIALS

saucepan and stove
½ cup salt
½ cup hot water
¼ cup cold water
½ cup cornstarch

wooden spoon
bowl
board
cookie sheet and oven, optional

PROCESS

1. Prepare the dough as follows:
   Mix the salt and hot water in the pan. Boil.
   Stir cold water into the cornstarch in a bowl.
   Add the cornstarch-water mixture to the boiled water and stir.
   Cook over low, stirring until the consistency is like pie dough.
   Pour out of the pan onto a board.
2. When cooled slightly, knead until smooth.
3. Explore the dough freely, creating objects or sculptures as desired.
4. The dough will harden in one to two days or can be speed dried on a cookie sheet in an oven set at 200°F for 1 hour or so.

Courtesy MaryAnn Kohl, 2021

Basic Bread Clay

Art by child, age 3.
Courtesy Jennifer Goodman Crowell of the Child Development Cooperative in Baton Rouge, LA

Bird by child, age 3.
Courtesy Jennifer Goodman Crowell of the Child Development Cooperative in Baton Rouge, LA

Bread clay isn't really bread, but the name has stuck because of its ingredients. This modeling dough is made with flour, salt, and water. It can be baked or air-dried, painted or colored, and is a very manageable modeling mixture. For a nice shine, coat the hardened art objects with white glue that has been thinned with water.

MATERIALS

4 cups flour	1 cup warm water, plus	floured surface	foil or waxed paper
1 cup salt	½ cup	plastic wrap	cookie sheet

PROCESS

1. Prepare the dough in a bowl: Mix 4 cups flour and 1 cup salt. Make a well in the center and pour in 1 cup warm water, mixing with the hands. Add ½ cup more of warm water and continue mixing. Clay should not be crumbly or sticky but should form a ball. Knead five minutes on a floured board until very smooth.
2. Work with a small portion of dough at a time, and wrap the remainder of the dough in plastic and place in the refrigerator. Hint: If dough dries out, add a few drops of water and knead into the dough until it is smooth again.
3. Work on a sheet of foil or waxed paper so the dough won't stick to the table and can be easily lifted from the backing. Create any kind of objects, letters, ornaments, and so forth.
4. When a sculpture is complete, bake it at 325°F on a cookie sheet for 1 hour or until hard. When tapped with a knife, the dough should not give but should sound hollow on both the top and the bottom.

EXTENSIONS

- Some suggestions to try after free exploration has been experienced:
  - beads
  - bugs, insects
  - jewelry
  - napkin rings
  - ornaments
  - picture frames
- Suggestions for making play food:
  - fruits
  - vegetables
  - cookies
  - baked goods
  - cupcakes
  - pretzels
  - hamburgers
- For a colored dough, add food coloring or paint into the ball of dough and knead the color in. Colored dough will appear lighter when baked or dried.

Shapes & Sticks

Choose a paper shape, and design and decorate it in any way. Collect all kinds of sticks. Then attach the decorated shape to a stick, and insert it in a Styrofoam block to give it a perch.

MATERIALS

construction paper, cut into any geometric shapes (square, circle, triangle, rectangle)
scissors
marking pens
tempera paints or liquid watercolors in shallow containers
paintbrushes
rags and jar of water

sticks: craft sticks, wooden ice-cream spoons, tongue depressors
other fun sticks: coffee stir sticks, pretzel sticks, twigs
joining tools: glue, stapler, tape
dowel, bamboo skewer, or wooden chopstick
Styrofoam block for display

Courtesy Sue Gaudnyski, Art in Miss G's Garden, 2021

PROCESS

1. Choose or cut a geometric paper shape about 3 inches across. Any manageable size is fine.
2. Design and decorate the shape with tempera paints, liquid watercolors, or marking pens. Imagination rules!
3. Glue craft sticks or wooden ice-cream spoons to the paper shape to add interesting and fun characteristics. Sticks can be painted too! Note: Liquid watercolors soak into craft sticks nicely and dry quickly.
4. Continue embellishing the paper shapes until satisfied.
5. With adult help, attach a long stick to the paper shape resembling a lollipop. Tape and staplers may both be needed, and glue will add additional strength when dry.
6. With adult help, stick the long stick into a Styrofoam block so the art will stand alone. If you don't have Styrofoam, a ball of air-dry dough or a scrap of wood with a small hole in it will suffice.

EXTENSIONS

- Add sparkly glitter, glitter glue, and sequins.
- Add pom-poms and cotton balls.
- Add googly eyes.
- Create puppets on sticks. Put on a puppet show.

Clay & Stick Sculpture

Roll balls of modeling clay, play clay, playdough, or other favorite dough. Create an engineering sculpture that grows and grows, with the balls as the joining medium. Join the balls with a choice of sticks, such as coffee stir sticks, toothpicks, drinking straws, or craft sticks. Use one kind of stick or combine many kinds. Build and build as far and wide as the artist desires!

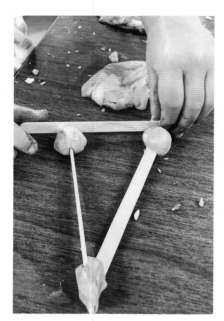

MATERIALS

dough or clay (see pages 138–139 for recipes)
selection of sticks: craft sticks, coffee stir sticks, toothpicks, chopsticks, drinking straws, bamboo skewers
base, optional: cardboard, paper plate, paper, wood scrap

PROCESS

1. Roll balls of the dough into a workable size, from the size of a cherry to the size of a golf ball. Make many balls! Save them for step 2.
2. Insert one end of a stick into a ball of dough and the other end of the same stick into another ball of dough. Now add another stick, repeating the steps and joining sticks and dough balls in a sculpture. The artwork can be small or large, depending on the thoughts of the artist. Some artists strive for *tall* while other artists strive for *long*. The results are always unique.
3. The sculpture can take shape on a base material, such as a piece of cardboard, or remain completely free of a base.
4. Some clays dry overnight for a permanent sculpture, while other doughs and clays will remain soft.

EXTENSIONS

Build a stick sculpture with other binding and stick materials such as the following:
- mini marshmallows and toothpicks
- full-size marshmallows and bamboo skewers (cut in half)
- gumdrops and toothpicks
- soft peas and toothpicks, dried overnight (soften dry peas in water before building)

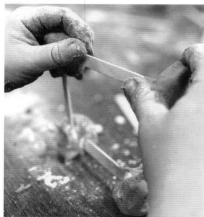

Art by child, age 7.
Courtesy Jennifer Goodman Crowell, 2021

6

Craft & Construction

Collage Construction

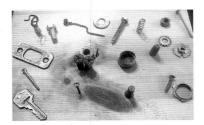

Art by Breanna Bode, age 6.
Courtesy Cathy Bode, 2021

Anything goes with open-ended construction! Attach well-chosen collage items to a plywood base. Add a hand drill, hammer, and screwdriver to increase the possibilities.

MATERIALS

base material: plywood square or thick (doubled) cardboard

collage items:

aluminum foil	clips	nails	screws
broken jewelry	corks	nuts, bolts, washers	small wood scraps
cardboard scraps	keys	paper scraps	soda flip-tops
chains	metal hooks	pipe cleaners	

tools: hand drill, hammer, screwdriver

glue, optional

scissors, optional

PROCESS

1. Set up a protected work space where nails or drilling wood will not harm the table or floor. Collage construction is an active art experience.
2. Collage items can be glued to the base. This is one method.
3. Some other methods to explore are:
   - hammer a nail directly into the base
   - hammer a nail through another item, such as a cardboard scrap, into the base
   - screw a wood screw with a screwdriver into the base
   - drill a hole, then stick an item, such as a pipe cleaner, in the hole
   - drill through a collage item, such as a small wood scrap, and attach to the base with a screw
   - drill a hole and hammer a bolt into the base
   - drill a hole and hammer a bolt with washers and nuts into the base
   - many more possibilities that artists will discover while creating

EXTENSIONS

- Paint or stain the wood base before beginning. Allow to dry completely.
- Draw on the wood base with a permanent marker. Follow the drawn lines when placing collage items on the base.

Courtesy Cathy Bode, 2021

Random Weaving

The beginning experience of weaving is as simple as wrapping yarn through small cuts in cardboard and watching the shapes, colors, and interaction of the yarns evolve and unfold in pattern and design. Adult help will be necessary when cutting mat board or cardboard.

MATERIALS

mat board or cardboard squares
scissors
yarn or embroidery floss

tape
decorative materials, optional: feathers, beads, buttons, stickers, bows

PROCESS

1. Start by cutting well-spaced slits in the sides of mat or cardboard squares. Make each slit about ½ inch deep and at least 1 inch apart, although there is no strict rule about the spacing. Cut on all four sides, or on two sides only. The artist chooses.
2. Pull one end of a piece of yarn through a slit so the end of the yarn is on the back of the mat board. Tape the end of the yarn to the back of the board if desired.
3. Begin wrapping the yarn from one slit to another, pulling the yarn tight through each slit. Yarn may crisscross, go front to back, around and over, through, or here and there. In other words, wrap yarn in any way desired.
4. Add more yarn by starting in any slit, even one that has already been used, and pull the end into the slit snugly. Begin wrapping again. Ends may be taped on the back of the mat board if desired.
5. If further decorating of the weaving is desired, add feathers or beads during or after the weaving. Many collage materials of your choice will be suitable for adding to the weaving.

Courtesy MaryAnn Kohl, 2021

EXTENSIONS

- Mat board may be cut in shapes other than squares, such as a circle, triangle, hexagon, diamond, heart, or oval. Oddly shaped, free-form shapes are interesting too. Try shapes with holes cut in their centers—or whatever the artist can imagine!
- Use markers to color in the areas between the yarn lines.
- Before weaving, cover mat board with fabric or wrapping paper.

Wonder Weaving

What can artists weave? What materials can they weave with? We wonder! Anything with holes or spaces becomes the beginning base for a wonder weaving: A fence. A wire rack. A plastic berry basket. A cardboard pizza circle. The list goes on.

Courtesy Sue Gaudnyski, Art in Miss G's Garden, 2021

MATERIALS

scissors and tape
weaving base that has a grid or spaces: fence, wire rack, cardboard pizza circle, laundry basket
materials to weave with:

colored wire	embroidery thread	pipe cleaners	sewing trims
construction tape	feathers	raffia	torn fabric strips
crepe paper	jute	ribbon	twine
crochet thread	lace	rope	yarn

PROCESS

With so many weaving possibilities, let's begin with cardboard pizza circles as an example:

1. Snip a cut into the edge of a cardboard pizza circle. Make the cut about 1 inch deep.
2. Make more cuts spaced around the edge of the circle. Every 2 inches works well, but there is no required spacing.
3. Begin the weaving by pulling a strand of regular yarn or twine through one of the cuts. Go straight across the circle, pull into the cut and then back to a different cut, then straight across again, back to a different cut, and so on until all the cuts have yarn inserted. This becomes the weaving base.

Courtesy Ronda Harbaugh, 2021

4. Take some thick yarn or sewing trim and begin the weaving. Go in and out of the yarn or twine in any pattern. Repeating a pattern helps make the weaving hold together well, but any pattern is welcome. If needed, use tape on the back of the circle to end one strand and start a new one. Strands can also be tied one to another to keep things going.
5. Fill the circle until it is thick with color and weaving materials. When satisfied with the weaving, think of something else to weave. What about a Hula-Hoop? A laundry basket?

EXTENSIONS

- Add collage materials to the weaving, such as beads, feathers, buttons, pipe cleaners, and paper scraps.
- A group of artists can work together to weave a chain-link fence with strips of torn fabric, caution tape, and other long pieces of material.

Hula-Hoop Mobile

Creating a mobile using a Hula-Hoop as the base is a great group activity. Everyone can pitch in and tie colorful strips of fabric and ribbon to the hoop. Add other colorful strands and trims until the hoop is full. Tying and knotting strips and strands is a great skill for kids to explore.

MATERIALS

long torn strips of fabric, about 1–2 inches wide
scissors
Hula-Hoop
long ribbons

long strands of thick yarn
long strands of sewing trims
more yarn or twine for hanging
hook for hanging the mobile, optional

PROCESS

1. Save fabric scraps and other strands of materials like ribbons, thick yarn, and sewing trims.
2. Tear fabric into strips. If the fabric won't tear easily, use scissors. Tearing enough strips for the mobile will be a big job, so everyone should pitch in.
3. Put all the strips and other strands in a shallow box or on a tray at the work space.
4. Begin by tying a strip of fabric to the Hula-Hoop. Tie with any knot that works. One simple technique is to double the strip, bend it over the hoop, and then pull the loose tails through the loop.
5. Work tying fabric strips, ribbons, yarn, and sewing trims to the Hula-Hoop until it is completely full. They do not have to be the same length but cutting all the strands the same length is a possibility.
6. To hang the hoop mobile, an adult can tie four equal lengths of twine or yarn to the Hula-Hoop, evenly spaced around the hoop. The strands should be longer than the diameter of the hoop, and long enough to join together well above the hoop. Tie the four strands together with a strong knot, and then hang the mobile from a hook, on a patio or deck, from a tree, or from a ceiling beam.

EXTENSIONS

- Create small mobiles using embroidery hoops, following the same basic directions as above.
- Tie strings to the Hula-Hoop. Then attach any number of objects, found or homemade, to the strings. Move the strings on the hoop to help the hoop balance, spreading out the weight of the objects so all the heavy ones are not just on one side of the hoop.

Courtesy Janine Kloiber, 2021

Craft & Construction | **119**

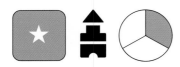

Colander Sculpture

Courtesy of Sunshine and Puddles Family Day Care, 2021

All those little colander holes are just begging to be filled with color and fun! Gather materials of choice, such as pipe cleaners and feathers, beads and buttons, straws and narrow sticks. A colander sculpture can go in oh-so-many directions, all of them worthwhile explorations for the youngest artists. A plus of the activity is that it can be easily disassembled and used once again, and the colander will continue to be a viable kitchen tool without damage.

MATERIALS

kitchen colander
glue and scissors, optional
sculpture materials:

art tissue	collage materials	pipe cleaners	sticks
bamboo skewers	faux flowers	pony beads	straws
buttons	feathers	scraps of paper	

PROCESS

1. Collect the sculpture material choices and spread them out on the work space with the colander, ready to go. Pipe cleaners are a must. Whatever other chosen materials are on hand will add to the creativity, color, and design.
2. Insert pipe cleaners into the holes in the colander. They can be straight, bent, looped, or cut into smaller lengths.
3. Craft beads and buttons with large holes can be threaded on pipe cleaners too.
4. Add other materials. Feathers and drinking straws work especially well.
5. Fill the colander until satisfied with the sculptural design.
6. The colander can be taken apart at a later time and used again for art and will continue to be useful in the kitchen.

EXTENSION

Create a natural-materials colander sculpture with items collected from outdoors. Some suggestions are:

- long grasses
- tall weeds
- flowers with long stems
- leaves with long stems
- twigs

Branch Weaving

Find a branch with "arms" growing out of it. Begin winding yarn from one arm of the branch to the next. Other yarns, fabric, and natural materials such as grasses, feathers, and weeds give the branch weaving a natural organic look.

MATERIALS

branch with at least 2 arms
heavy yarn, variety of colors
scissors
natural materials: grasses, wool, feathers, cotton, weeds, flowers
weaving materials:

embroidery thread	newspaper strips	ribbon
fabric strips	paper strips	sewing trims and scraps
leather strips	raffia	shoelaces

Art by Ellie Harney, age 7.
Courtesy of Megan Harney, ourhandcraftedlife.com, 2021

PROCESS

1. Cut yarn into 3-foot lengths, usually a manageable length. Wrap yarn from one arm of the branch to another, creating multiple lines of yarn between the arms. Other weaving materials will use this beginning wrapped yarn as the base for the weaving. Tie a knot or loop the yarn around the branch to start the wrapping. If running out of yarn, simply add more.

2. When all the yarn has been wrapped from arm to arm and holds strong, begin weaving other materials such as grasses, wool, weeds, and more yarns and fabrics through the beginning yarn strands. Weave and tuck materials into the first wrapping of yarn. Weave over, under, and through, or weave in any fashion that holds. Note: some artists will weave a very random design while others will try for a pattern.

EXTENSIONS

- Wrap a single stick with yarns and fabrics to create a woven stick.
- Find a grapevine wreath and weave and wrap materials through it.
- Cut slits around a cardboard pizza circle and make a large circle weaving.

Flowers in Cardboard

Poke holes in a piece of cardboard or a strong paper plate. Then fill the holes with flowers, weeds, grasses, and other natural items from the outdoors. Be sure to ask permission before picking living flowers or plants.

MATERIALS

base material: cardboard box, heavy paper plate, cardboard pizza circle
flowers, weeds, grasses, and other natural items
scissors

PROCESS

1. To begin, an adult pokes holes in the chosen piece of cardboard or paper plate. A Phillips screwdriver pokes holes reasonably safely. Scissors poke holes too but are a little harder to control. Be cautious.
2. Go for a walk outdoors in one's own yard, a park, or a friend's property with permission. Collect growing things that are permissible to pick or cut. Keep stems long if possible. Scissors can help snip stems so the roots are not pulled up from the ground.

3. Insert each flower stem or other natural item into a hole in the cardboard. Fill the cardboard until puffy and colorful.
4. When indoors again, some artists choose to float the cardboard and plants in a baking dish filled with water. Still others prefer to pull the items from the board and place them in a vase with water.

EXTENSIONS

- Draw a vase on a piece of cardboard. Poke holes just above the vase drawing. When flowers are inserted in the holes, it will look like they are in a vase.
- Draw a person's face or a pet's face on cardboard. Then insert plant materials—for example, daisy eyes, grass hair, berry lips, and a leaf nose.

Art by Clio, age 6.
Courtesy MaryAnn Kohl, 2021

Art by child, age 4.
Courtesy of Amy Kay, Miss Kay's Atelier, 2021.

Sewing Boards

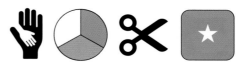

Making sewing boards has no age limit, and there is no boundary to the creative possibilities of sewing and lacing on cardboard with varieties of colorful threads, yarns, and ribbons. Add marking pen designs for an even more colorful experience.

MATERIALS

sewing board material: cardboard, mat board, strong paper plate
heavy-duty hole punch
yarn
masking tape
marking pens, optional

PROCESS

1. Punch holes in the mat board or cardboard with a heavy-duty hole punch. Adult help will be needed if the cardboard is very thick. Punch the holes in any pattern all around the edges of the board.
2. Wrap the end of a piece of yarn with masking tape to make a sturdy point. Begin sewing the yarn in and out of the holes, across the board, and in any direction. The yarn sewing and lacing work may resemble weaving.
3. Change yarn by tying or taping the next piece of yarn to the first, or tape the ends to the back of the board.
4. When complete, tape or tie the last end of yarn to the back of the board.
5. Add colorful marking pen drawings or color between the yarn designs if desired.

EXTENSIONS

- Use other materials for sewing boards such as:
  - – sewing trim
  - – ribbon
  - – lace
  - – thread
  - – embroidery floss
  - – crochet thread
  - – raffia
  - – elastic
- Glue a magazine picture, photograph, colored paper, or wrapping paper to the board first. Then punch the holes and design with yarn as before.

Art by Breanna, age 6.
Courtesy of Cathy Bode, 2021

Design Boards

Courtesy Sue Gaudnyski, Art in Miss G's Garden, 2021

Art by child, age 5.
Courtesy MaryAnn Kohl, 2021

Courtesy Sue Gaudnyski, Art in Miss G's Garden, 2021

Hammering and nailing as art may be a new thought for some artists, but when additional art materials are added, the artistic experience is one of the more imaginative yet accessible projects for all kids. Prepare for some loud pounding and creative approaches to sculpture.

MATERIALS

square of wood (8 by 8 inches works well) or a two-by-four
nails with wide heads
hammer
worktable
materials for stringing on the nails: rubber bands,
    sewing trims, yarn, floss, thread, raffia, string, ribbons
collage items: feathers, drinking straws, buttons, beads, stickers,
    cotton balls, pipe cleaners, macaroni

PROCESS

1. Hammer nails with large, flat heads into the wood in any design. Be careful nails do not go all the way through into the table or floor. Short nails help solve the problem.
2. Weave, tie, stretch, and connect the nails with colored threads, yarn, rubber bands, or other chosen materials.
3. Add or weave other collage items into the design board.
4. Materials can be removed and the board redesigned, or the original design can be saved or displayed.

EXTENSIONS

- Cover the wood board with fabric, paint, or wallpaper before adding the nails.
- Rubber bands stretched on the nails creates a design that can be removed and used over and over again.
- Draw rubber band designs on pieces of paper, and then copy the designs on the board.
- Add small pieces of wood scraps or picture frame pieces glued on the design board.
- Make a nails-only collage, page 125.

Nails-Only Collage

A nail collage needs nothing more for creativity and art exploration than a piece of wood for the base, a hammer, and a bucket of nails of all types. Take advantage of the texture, height, color, and shine of different kinds of nails to achieve design and visual impact.

MATERIALS

base wood piece, about 8 by 8 inches (any size or shape is fine, even driftwood)
hammer
nails in all sizes
worktable

PROCESS

1. Hammer the nails into the wood square.
2. Think about using the highs and lows of nail heights as part of the design. The sizes of the nail heads will add to the design too. Some nails are black, and some are silvery; others are gray or white.
3. Nails can be very close together or spaced farther apart. The collage design is completely up to the artist.

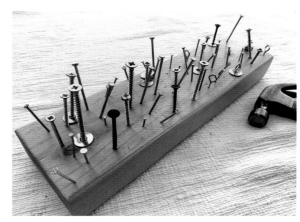

Art by Montessori group, ages 3 to 10.
Courtesy Jeanne Elser Smith, 2021

4. When the collage is complete, the nails can be pulled out again (some artists really enjoy dismantling the nails), or the nail collage can be saved as is.

EXTENSIONS

- Add other items into the collage such as those found in Design Board on page 124. Add screws, nuts, bolts, and other hardware.
- Cover the finished nails-only collage with aluminum foil, with nails poking through or with nails making a bumpy design under the foil.
- Cover the board before beginning with foil, paint, paper, or fabric.

Easy Yarn Suncatcher

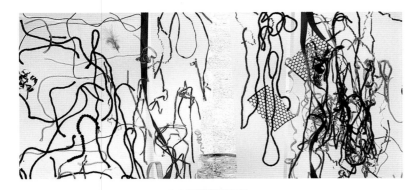

Clear, adhesive contact paper becomes a light-filled canvas for colorful yarn designs. Tape a piece of peeled contact paper to a window, sticky side facing the artist. The artist sticks strands of yarn to the contact paper in any designs or patterns. No glue needed! Perfect for the youngest artist in the room, but teens love this too. See the light shine through the colorful art.

MATERIALS

clear adhesive contact paper   tape
scissors   yarn strands, many colors

PROCESS

1. An adult can cut a sheet of clear, adhesive contact paper from the roll. Sizes are not definite, but 8 by 10 inches is a good size. Peel off and discard the backing. Tape the contact paper to a window at child height, sticky side facing the artist (not facing the window).
2. Place yarn strands in a basket or tub next to the window. Keep the length short and manageable for younger artists. Many colors, thicknesses, and textures are inspiring!
3. Scissors can be kept handy for snipping yarn to add to creativity and exploration.
4. The artist stands at the window and attaches yarn to the sticky contact paper. Yarn can be pressed on and pulled off without problem. No glue is needed.
5. The artist can work until satisfied. Then take a look at the light shining through the art! Leave the art on the window for several days to enjoy.

EXTENSION

Add other materials to the yarn suncatcher, such as pieces of art tissue, flower petals, leaves, stickers, and doilies—or whatever is on hand that inspires.

Art by child, age 3.
Courtesy Brittany Benner Dusek, 2021

PeekaBoo Treasure Jar

Fill a jar with uncooked rice. Then add some small treasures, such as coins, beads, sequins, broken jewelry parts, toy parts, or scrabble tiles. Tightly secure the lid with glue or duct tape. Turn it this way and that to see the hidden treasures appear.

MATERIALS

small items and treasures: coins, pom-poms, buttons, beads, confetti, alphabet beads, tiny toys, scrabble tiles, novelty erasers, broken jewelry parts, small charms, small faux flowers
glass jar or clear plastic bottle with lid
uncooked rice to fill the container
glue or duct tape

Courtesy Trisha Thompson, 2021

PROCESS

1. Collect small treasures over time. Place a selection of the treasures on a tray. The artist can sort and investigate before beginning with the rice and other steps.
2. When ready, pour an inch or two of rice into the container, leaving room for more.
3. Drop several treasures into the jar on the rice.
4. Add more rice to cover the treasures. Then add several more treasures.
5. Finish with rice, leaving some space so rice and treasures can move around when the jar is shaken, tilted, tipped, or rolled.
6. Squeeze a small amount of glue in the lid to cover the inside edges, and then tighten the lid on the jar. The glue will need to dry overnight. Duct tape is another secure choice.
7. Meanwhile, roll the jar this way and that to see all the treasures peeking out of the rice. The more the jar is turned and joggled, tilted and tipped, held upside down and then right side up again, the more the rice and treasures will mix and move. Treasures disappear and reappear. Peekaboo!

Courtesy Melea Martin, 2021

EXTENSIONS

- Design a theme treasure jar with specially selected items. Some ideas are: coins, holiday, birthday, nature, sports.
- Add glitter and sequins to the rice.
- Dried beans, peas, or lentils can replace rice and add color. Any of these can be mixed with the rice.

Contact Tissue Art

Courtesy Vicky Perreault, MessforLess.net, 2021

Montessori Land-Air-Water Art Exploration by children, ages 3 to 6. Courtesy Jeanne Elser Smith, 2021

Sticking tissue without the mess of glue or drying time is an instantly creative, enlivened art experience. Clear, adhesive contact paper becomes the bonding medium and colorful art tissue the design medium. Add scissors and some imaginative experimentation, and the project is ready to go. Contact paper can be unruly, so don't worry about perfection. Wrinkles, bubbles, and gaps are common, especially for younger artists or artists new to the medium.

MATERIALS

clear, adhesive contact paper, about 8 by 10 inches
scissors
art tissue scraps and squares

spoon, optional
hole punch
strand of yarn

PROCESS

1. Cut a workable size of clear contact paper from the roll, about 8 by 10 inches is typically manageable (any similar size is fine).
2. Pull back half of the protective backing on the contact paper. Press or fold it back, leaving the clear sticky half faceup.
3. Cut or tear art tissue into shapes or designs or use scraps of art tissue as found. Stick each one to the clear contact paper, pressing gently. Create a design, pattern, or random covering. Cover the sticky contact paper well.
4. When complete, pull the remaining protective backing completely off. Then fold this clear side over the decorated side and press the two together like a sandwich. Press with hands and smooth the surface. Rubbing the surface with the rounded side of a spoon brightens the art.
5. Use scissors to trim edges or round the corners. Snip or punch a little hole in the top of the design for a piece of yarn to slot through if the design will be hung in a window or other display area. Expect lumps and wrinkles in the contact paper.

EXTENSIONS

- Combine other art materials in the contact paper work such as dried weeds and flowers, doilies, lace, crayon shavings, glitter, feathers, yarn, sand, or confetti.
- Create other colorful ideas. Some suggestions are: holiday ornaments, mobiles, suncatchers.

Tissue Container

Colored art tissue comes in a rainbow of colors. Saved scraps of art tissue from other art experiences can come in handy for this activity. Glue art tissue to glass to create a translucent vase, bank, lantern, or pencil jar. The tissue covering helps prevent the glass from breaking. Worried about glass? A plastic container works equally well. Place the finished project in a sunny window to enjoy the look of stained glass.

Courtesy Leanne Durbin, 2021

MATERIALS

glass or plastic jar, vase, or bottle
newspaper
thinned white glue in a cup (liquid starch also
    works well)

paintbrush
colored art tissue scraps and pieces
clear hobby coating and brush, optional

PROCESS

1. Place the container right side up on a newspaper or other protective table covering.
2. Brush an area of the container with a mixture of white glue and water (or liquid starch). Stick a torn or cut piece of art tissue on the sticky area. Brush over the piece with more glue or starch.
3. Add more pieces of tissue, overlapping the edges, and sticking down all the edges. Stick tissue pieces over the edge of the mouth of the jar too. Let dry briefly. Then turn the jar over and finish by covering the base of the jar.
4. Dry overnight or until the tissue pieces are hard and translucent.
5. When the container is dry, an adult may cover it with a glaze of clear hobby coating for shine and protection, but this is not required. Dry again.

EXTENSIONS

- Turn the jar into a bank. To do this, an adult can cut a slot in the jar lid by hammering a chisel point into the lid to make a coin-sized slot. Then hammer the other side of the lid to flatten the raw edges of the slot. Start saving!
- Place a battery-powered votive candle in the jar. It will glow like stained glass!

- Add other types of materials to the container surface, such as small paper scraps, bits of doilies, yarn or thread, confetti, or pieces of flowers and weeds.
- Use art tissue and thinned glue on wood scraps, bottles, rocks, glass in a picture frame, waxed paper, or clear plastic wrap.

Courtesy Larissa Halfond, 2021

Colorful Curly Tubes

Courtesy MaryAnn Kohl, 2021

Collect any scrap paper you have on hand—construction paper, magazine pictures, craft paper—to make a curly tube sculpture. Artists experiment with manipulating the paper to make a new shape. Curly them up, and the tube design is ready to roll!

MATERIALS

paper scraps, with solid colors and patterned designs:

catalog pages	copying paper	magazine pictures
coloring book pages	drawing paper	newspaper
construction paper	junk mail	patterned craft paper

pencil

square base: thick paper, cardboard, or wood

scissors

glue

PROCESS

1. Collect an assortment of scrap paper in many colors and patterns. Select a scrap of paper to make the first paper curl. The scrap can be a square, a long strip, a rectangle, or any shape at all.
2. Roll the scrap around a pencil. Roll it tight and hold briefly to encourage the curl. Then let it go. The scrap is now a curled tube!
3. Put a small puddle of glue on the cardboard or wood base. Stick the curled tube in a standing position in the glue. It should stay in place as it dries.
4. Continue making curled tubes, standing each one on the cardboard base. They can all be the same height or cut to be different heights. The placement can be random or planned. It's up to the artist to decide.
5. Allow the curly tubes to dry overnight.
6. There are many ways to display this sculpture, including on the wall, on a shelf, hanging upside down, or in a group with several other curly tube artworks.

EXTENSIONS

- Add collage materials of choice to further design the curly tube artworks. Buttons, beads, yarn, and so forth will add color and design to the sculpture.

- Add a small faux flower in each tube.
- Add pompoms, glitter, or sequins.

Festive Banner

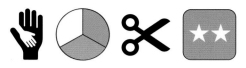

What better way is there to decorate and brighten a room than with a banner painted with festive colors? Keep a supply of finished banners ready to decorate and celebrate special days, holidays, or seasons.

MATERIALS

bright paper, about 11 by 14 inches or larger
two thin sticks, a bit wider than the paper
stapler or glue
tempera paints in cups

paintbrushes
string, twine, or yarn
newspaper or protective table covering

PROCESS

1. Staple or glue the sticks to the bright paper, one at the top and one at the bottom. Paint stir sticks from a craft store work great. These become the weight that keeps the banner hanging flat.
2. Using tempera paints, create designs, patterns, or pictures on the banner. Some artists like to write words as well.
3. Dry completely.
4. Tie string at both ends of the stick at the top of the banner.
5. Hang the banner from this string on the wall or other chosen area.

EXTENSIONS

- Use other coloring mediums to decorate the banner, such as fabric pens, paints, chalk, or crayons.
- Experiment with stencils, veggie prints, glitter, or other decorative ideas.
- Make an assortment of banners to change monthly or seasonally, celebrating the seasons or holidays through banner display.

Art by Zekiel, age 4.
Courtesy Mary Turner, Mimi's House Family Childcare, 2021

Pressed Flowers

Courtesy Jeanne Elser Smith, 2021

Pressed flowers and plants are delicate and lovely, lending themselves to infinite creative arrangements. There is a waiting period of about two to four weeks for the pressing of the plants to take place. When pressed and dry, glue them in designs or arrangements on paper, just like painting a beautiful picture.

MATERIALS

fresh greenery: flowers, blossoming
   weeds, ferns, grasses, evergreen
   twigs, leaves
newspaper
heavy books or heavy objects

tweezers
glue in a dish
toothpicks
heavy paper

PROCESS

1. Go for a walk and collect fresh flowers or blossoming weeds, such as buttercups, chamomile, and daisies, as well as leaves, ferns, and lacy grasses. Every part of the earth offers a unique variety of natural flowers and plants. (Be cautious of plants that poke or sting. Be mindful of permissions and private property. An adult should supervise.)
2. Spread the plants out on newspaper with space between each one. The flowers and plants should not touch. Place several more sheets of newspaper on top of them.
3. Place books or heavy objects on top of the paper which will cause the plants and flowers to flatten as they are pressed. The hard part: Wait for two to four weeks for the plants to thoroughly dry out, keeping in mind that thicker plants take the longest.
4. Remove the heavy books, peel back the newspaper, and carefully handle the delicate, dried pressed flowers, weeds, and leaves. Tweezers are helpful.
5. Dip a toothpick in the white glue and touch it to the heavy paper, making a dot of glue. Then pick up a dried flower with fingers or with tweezers and place it on the glue dot. Add other dried blossoms and flowers to make an arrangement on the paper. Dry completely.

EXTENSIONS

- On a rectangle of peeled clear contact paper, stick and arrange dried flower petals or leaves. Press another layer of contact paper over this. Rub to remove bubbles. Punch a hole and thread yarn through the hole. This is a great way to make a bookmark.
- Pretty note cards can be made with dried pressed flowers and leaves.

Natural Sculpture

Collect items from nature throughout the year, and save them for creating a sculpture. Use lots of glue and a good, sturdy base so the sculpture can be filled to overflowing with the natural collection.

MATERIALS

extraheavy cardboard circle or square for a base
scissors
materials from nature: pine cones, nuts, dried leaves, dried grasses, seed pods, moss, thistles, twigs, weeds

glue (or glue gun, with adult supervision)
raffia, ribbon, or sewing trims, optional
clear hobby paint, optional

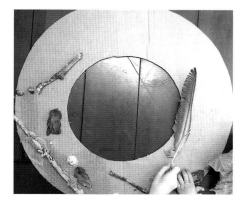

PROCESS

1. Choose a cardboard base. If you cut a circle and then cut another smaller circle from the center, the finished art can be a wreath. (A cardboard pizza circle makes a good base.)
2. Glue materials from nature to the cardboard, one by one. Use a generous amount of glue. A glue gun can be used with adult supervision.
3. Fill the cardboard until the cardboard backing no longer shows through. This may take some time. Wrap, tie, or glue other optional decorating materials, such as ribbon or raffia, to the sculpture.
4. Dry overnight or longer on a flat surface. The sculpture or wreath must be completely dry before hanging or using as a centerpiece. When dry, an adult may spray the sculpture with a clear hobby coating for a glossy effect, but this is not required.

EXTENSIONS

- Enjoy the circle sculpture as a table centerpiece. Place a battery-operated candle in the center.
- Work with materials such as holiday decorations, tinsel, glitter, confetti, or gold-and-silver-sprayed pine cones and pasta.
- Make a theme sculpture or wreath from recycled materials and objects:
  - hardware
  - toy parts
  - recycled mail
  - family photos
  - hair rollers
  - food

Art by Breanna, age 6.
Courtesy Cathy Bode, 2021

Painted Sticks Sculpture

Community project by Montessori students, ages 3 to 6.
Courtesy Jeanne Elser Smith, 2021

Courtesy Melea Martin, 2021

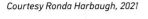

Courtesy Ronda Harbaugh, 2021

These two methods for painting sticks offer two ways to create a unique sculpture or an artistic hanging. Find sticks in nature or use wooden craft sticks. How the sticks are painted will be what allows them to burst into color and design.

MATERIALS

natural sticks or craft sticks
tempera paints
paint brushes (method 1)

jars of various heights (method 2)
jar of water, rag
string or yarn and tree (method 1)
cardboard base and glue (method 2)

PROCESS

Method 1: Sticks from Nature

1. Collect sticks from the outdoors. Brush them off if needed. Leave the bark as found, or peel away dry bark. Assemble the sticks on the work space.
2. Arrange tempera paints and brushes on the work space with a jar of water for rinsing brushes. Paint the sticks with tempera paints and brushes. Rinse the brushes often to keep colors bright and pure. Use a rag to dry brushes a little if needed.
3. When the paint dries, tie yarn or string to each stick and hang each one from a tree, creating an outdoor tree sculpture. Sticks could also be hung from a gazebo or patio roof.

Method 2: Craft Stick Dipping

1. Assemble craft sticks on the work space. Pour tempera paints into containers of various heights, from very short to medium-tall. The taller the container, the more the paint will cover the sticks. Shorter containers? Less coverage of paint on the sticks.
2. Dip a craft stick into tempera paint in one of the containers. Allow extra paint to drip off, and then place the painted stick on the cardboard rectangle base. Continue dipping sticks in paint and arranging them on the cardboard rectangle together.
3. The sticks should adhere to the cardboard without glue, but if needed, add a big dot of glue on the back of each stick and return it to its original place on the cardboard.
4. Allow the art to dry overnight. When dry, lift up the cardboard and make sure all the sticks are adhering well. If not, add glue.
5. The cardboard with colorful sticks will make a wall hanging or can be displayed tilted upright on a shelf or windowsill.

Wooden Spoon Puppet

A trip to the dollar store or a yard sale is an inexpensive way to find wooden spoons or wooden spatulas. Googly eyes are a must for these puppets! As the saying goes, "Never enough googly eyes!" Put out markers, yarn, feathers, and other collage materials to give the puppet personality. A puppet show will be the natural spin-off.

MATERIALS

wooden spoon or flat wooden spatula
glue
scissors
materials and collage items:

buttons	paints and brushes
fabric scraps	pompoms
faux fur	ribbon
flower blossoms, artificial	sequins and spangles
glitter glue	stickers
googly eyes (stick-on or glue-on)	washi tape
markers	yarn

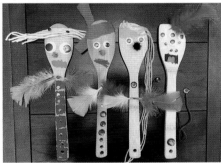

Art by Amalia Goodfriend, age 4; Josephine Kloiber, age 4; and Leonard Kloiber, age 6.
Courtesy Janine Kloiber, 2021

PROCESS

1. Spread out a collection of materials for decorating wooden spoons and transforming them into puppets. Use items from the list above or find other ideas of what will work best.
2. How many eyes does a puppet have? There is no firm answer. Googly eyes will abound!
3. Add materials to bring the puppet's personality to life. If glue is needed, allow time for drying.
4. Artists often wish to have a puppet show.

EXTENSIONS

- Cut a puppet shape from cardboard and decorate as desired. Add a loop of masking tape on the back to act as a handle for the puppeteer or glue the puppet to a cardboard rectangle as a handle.
- Sew and glue materials to a clean used sock to create a sock puppet.

Chopstick Stack Sculpture

Stick a chopstick into a ball of air-dry clay, making a strong base for the sculpture. Stack materials on the chopstick, using paper or foil cupcake liners, balls of dough, cut drinking straws, slices of cardboard tubes, and more. Build it tall and colorful or short and puffy. Being inventive is part of the fun.

MATERIALS

chopsticks (bamboo skewers are an alternative)
air-dry dough: recipe on page 138, or a commercial air-dry product
scissors, hole punch, craft-shape punches
materials to stack on or decorate the chopstick:

art tissue scraps	drinking straws, in short sections	ribbons
cupcake liners, paper and foil	cardboard tubes, in short sections	yarn
construction paper scraps	fabric scraps	macaroni
air-dry clay, small balls	felt scraps	

glue, optional
markers
glitter glue

Courtesy Natalie Valentine, 2021

PROCESS

1. Begin by making the air-dry clay. Cool slightly. You can also use a commercial air-dry product.
2. Form some of the clay into a ball and press it on the work space to flatten the bottom of the ball. This will become a strong, nontip base when it is dry. Make as many clay bases as you need. Before drying the clay, stick a chopstick into the center of a clay ball. Dry in place.
3. Start stacking materials on the chopstick, such as cupcake liners and drinking straw sections. Build it high or build it short. Punching or poking holes in solid materials may be necessary. Wrapping the chopstick with yarn or ribbons is also a technique that works well. Explore, discover, and experiment.
4. When the stacking is complete, check the clay base, making sure the stick is secure in the clay. Add some glue in the hole if you think it's needed.

EXTENSION

Drill a hole in a block of wood for a base. Insert the chopstick or a dowel in the hole, and start stacking. Use a little glue to make the connection of the stick in the hole strong.

Resources

Quick Recipe and Formula Guide

Air-Dry Dough
1 cup cornstarch
2 cups baking soda
1½ cups water
Stir all three ingredients in a pot. Food coloring can be added. Cook on medium or low heat for a few minutes. Knead and roll flat, or use for small sculptures. Excellent air-dry dough.

Baker's Clay
4 cups flour
1 cup salt
1¾ cups warm water
This recipe is versatile, soft, pliable, and dries well—either in the oven or air-dried. If a colored dough is desired, add food coloring, liquid watercolors, or tempera paint to the water before combining. Mix ingredients in a bowl. Knead for 5 to 10 minutes. Model objects and sculptures. Bake at 300°F for 1 to 3 hours, or air dry for a few days. Glaze with egg white, evaporated milk, or mayonnaise before baking. Or paint with a clear varnish or fixative after baking and cooling.

Bread Clay
⅔ cup warm water
½ cup salt
2 cups flour
Mix water and salt in a bowl. Add flour and stir. Knead. Model and explore dough. Bake dough objects 225°F–250°F for 4 to 6 hours. Objects should be hard on both sides.

Bubble Print
Mix a solution of equal parts water and liquid dish detergent. Let stand overnight. Glycerin can be added but is not required.

Chalk and Sugar Water
½ cup water
2 tablespoons sugar
Stir together until dissolved. Dip chalk into sugar-water mixture and then draw or color. Drawings are bright and less smudgy, but they still smudge some.

Cornstarch Beads
¾ cup flour
½ cup cornstarch
½ cup salt
food coloring or powdered tempera, if desired
⅜ cup warm water
Mix all dry ingredients in a bowl. Then add water gradually. Knead, adding a dusting of flour to help prevent dough from sticking to the hands. Pinch pieces for beads, roll into balls, and pierce each bead with a plastic darning needle, straw, or toothpick. Dry for a few days. Sometimes holes need to be repierced. Dough stays colorful when dry. Beads may be coated with a clear enamel when dry.

Finger Paints #1
Put liquid starch and powdered or liquid tempera paint directly on the paper and mix by hand. Then finger paint.

Finger Paints #2
Boil 3 parts water and remove from heat. Dissolve 1 part cornstarch in a little cold water, and then add to the hot water, stirring constantly. Boil until clear and thick. Add tempera paint, food coloring, or liquid watercolors. Use while warm or cool.

Slick Surface Paint
½ cup of tempera paint powder
1 teaspoon liquid dishwashing detergent
For paint to adhere to aluminum foil, cottage cheese containers, yogurt cups, frozen meal trays, mix this up for a thick paint. Test the paint on foil or plastic. If it does not stick, add about ½ teaspoon more of dishwashing liquid. Adding dishwashing liquid to any paint will help it adhere to slippery surfaces.

Glue, Thinned with Water
Squeeze some white glue (Elmer's School Glue is a common brand) into a jar or dish and mix in water with a paintbrush until the glue is thin and paints easily with a brush on paper. Tempera paint, liquid watercolors, or food coloring can be added to thinned glue to make a colored glue.

Goop
Mix two parts cornstarch with one part water in a pan. Use hands, spoons, and cups to explore Goop.

Pasta, Colored

Mix food coloring with cold water. Place dry pasta into the dye, swirl it around, and then remove the pasta, placing it on a thick pad of newspaper to dry. Move the pasta about while drying so it won't stick to the paper. You may wish to wear rubber gloves during this entire process.

Playdough

1 cup flour
1 cup water
1 cup salt
1 tablespoon cream of tartar

Mix and cook on low in a pan until a ball forms. Leave natural or color with food coloring, tempera paint, Kool-Aid, Jell-O, or liquid watercolor paint. Knead and then use warm or cool. Store in an airtight container.

Puffy Paint Dough

Mix equal parts of flour, salt, and water to form a paste. Separate dough into bowls and add powdered tempera paint to each one. Then place the colored dough into squeeze bottles. Squeeze onto heavy paper like frosting. Do not eat.

Salt Cornstarch Dough

½ cup salt
½ cup hot water
¼ cup cold water
½ cup cornstarch
food coloring or tempera paint

Add color to water. Mix everything over low heat, stirring until the mixture is too stiff to stir. When cool, knead until smooth. Model. Dry. Paint.

Salt Modeling Dough

1 part salt
1 part flour

Mix in a bowl. Add enough water to make a thick frosting-like dough (about ⅔ part water). Stir. Color can be added now with food coloring or paint. Spread mixture on cardboard for maps or dioramas, making hills and valleys. Dry for one to two days. Paint and/or decorate when dry.

Sawdust Dough #1

Mix 4 cups sawdust, 1 cup wheat paste, and 2½ cups of water together. Paint or color is optional. Model. Dry.

Sawdust Dough #2

Mix 2 cups sawdust and 1 cup flour. Then add water until the dough is squishy and stiff. Knead. Model. Sand and paint, optional.

Soda Cornstarch Dough

1 cup cornstarch
2 cups baking soda
1⅓ cups water

Mix in a pan over medium heat, stirring constantly until thick like dough. Food coloring may be worked in when cooled slightly on a breadboard or piece of foil. Keep covered. Roll, cut, and model small shapes.

Starch, Homemade Liquid

Dissolve 1 teaspoon granulated starch in a little bit of water. Stir and add 1 cup hot water. Bring this to a boil for about 1 minute, stirring constantly. When cool, store in a container with an airtight lid. Lasts a long time.

Wallpaper Paste

4 cups flour
1 cup sugar
1 gallon water

Mix flour and sugar. Add enough water to make a smooth paste, about 1 gallon. Boil on the stove, stirring until thick and clear. Then thin with 1 quart cold water. Add oil of cinnamon to keep paste fresh smelling. Use with papier-mâché projects.

Collage Materials List

A
acorns
aluminum foil
apple seeds
apricot seeds
aquarium gravel

B
ball bearings
balsa wood
bamboo
bark
basket
beads
beans
bias tape
bobby pins
bolts and nuts
bones
bottle caps
bottles
brads
braiding
buckles
burlap scraps

C
cellophane
cellophane tape
chains
chalk
checkers
cloth scraps
clothespins
cloves
coffee filters
coffee grounds
coins
comb

confetti
construction
   paper scraps
contact paper
cord
corks
corn husks
corn kernels
costume jewelry
cotton
cotton balls
cotton swab
crepe paper
crystals

D
dice
dominoes
dried beans and
   peas
dried flowers
dried grass
dried seeds
driftwood
dry cereals

E
Easter grass
egg cartons
eggshells
elastic
embroidery floss
emery boards
erasers
evergreens
excelsior

F
fishing lures
flashbulbs

florist's foil
flowers, artificial
flowers, dried
flowers, fresh
flowers, plastic
foam
foam packing
foil, aluminum
foil, wrapping
   paper
fur samples

G
gauze
glass beads
glass mosaic
   pieces
glitter
gold jewelry parts
gold thread
grains
grasses
gravel
gummed paper
   reinforcements

H
hair netting
hair roller
hairpins
hardware scraps
hat trimmings
hooks

I J K L
inner tube scraps
jewelry pieces
jewelry wire
junk, all kinds
key rings

key tabs
keys
lemon seeds
lids

M
magazine pictures
mailing tubes
map pins
marbles
meal trays, paper
meal trays, plastic
meal trays,
   Styrofoam
metal scraps
metal shavings
mirrors
mosquito netting
moss, dried

N
nails
newspaper
noodles, dry and
   wet
nut cups
nuts

O
oilcloth scraps
orange seeds
orange sticks
origami paper
ornaments,
   holiday/seasonal

P
paint chips
paper baking cups
paper clips

paper dots
paper fasteners
paper products,
   all kinds
paper tubes
pasta
peach pits
pebbles
photocopies
photographs
pill bottles
pillboxes
pine cones
pine needles
Ping-Pong
   balls
pins, all kinds
pipe cleaners
plastic, all kinds
pumpkin seeds

Q R
quills
raffia
recording tape
reeds
rhinestones
ribbon
rice
rickrack
rock salt
rocks
rope pieces
rubber bands
rubber tubing

S
safety pins
salt crystals

sandpaper
sawdust
scouring pads
screening, plastic
   or wire
screws
seals, gummed
seam binding
seashells
seedpods
seeds
sequins
sewing tape
shelf liner
shoelaces
shot
silk scraps
skewers, bamboo
soap
soldering wire
spaghetti
sponges
spools
spray-can lids
stamps, all kinds
stars, stick on
steel wool
stickers
sticks
stones

T
tape, cellophane
tape, duct
tape, library
tape, masking
tape, mystic
tape, plastic

tape, Scotch
tape, sewing
telephone wire
thistles
thread
tiles
tinker-toy parts
tissue paper
tongue depressors
toothbrushes
toothpicks
torn paper scraps
toys, broken/
   orphaned
twigs
twine

U V W
velvet scraps
wallpaper
warp
washers
wax candles
weeds
wood scraps
wood shavings
wooden beads
wooden dowels
wooden wheels
wool
wrapping papers

X Y Z
X-rays
yarns
zippers

Index

About the Author

As a child growing up in Longmeadow, Massachusetts, in the 1950s, young MaryAnn Faubion enjoyed art, music, reading, and playing outside. Her most treasured possessions were a box of pastel chalks, her Indian Princess bicycle with a generator for headlights, and a Ginny doll with adorable outfits (including ice-skates).

In high school, MaryAnn added working on the yearbook staff and cheerleading to her interests. She continued to ride her bike, draw, and let's not forget babysitting at 50¢ an hour. Dating also took on a new importance as did driving her first car.

In 1968 MaryAnn married Michael Kohl and moved to Virginia where she received a BS in Education from Old Dominion University, Norfolk, Virginia, and later moved back to the Pacific Northwest and received a graduate degree from Western Washington University, Bellingham, Washington, in Elementary Education, English, Speech, and Drama. Her favorite college classes were music education, art education, and Greek mythology.

After years teaching elementary education, MaryAnn retired to raise her two daughters. Both are now grown and in theatre and visual arts. She gradually began to write art books for children while teaching art workshops, and founded her own publishing company, Bright Ring Publishing. Writing took on new importance in her daily life and continues to this day.

She still loves to draw, read, write, ride her bike when she finds the time, and drive her favorite car. Playing with her pup Frances is a daily delight. She and her granddaughters love to play with her Ginny dolls and pastel chalks. She lives in the Pacific Northwest on a rocky beach in the shadow of a volcano.